The Content Pool

Pool

Leverage Your Company's Largest Hidden Asset

Alan J. Porter

The Content Pool

Leverage Your Company's Largest Hidden Asset

Copyright © 2012 Alan J. Porter

Graphics Credits

Cover Design and Illustrations: Douglas Potter

Disclaimer

Trademarks

XML Press
Laguna Hills, California
http://xmlpress.net

First Edition
ISBN: 978-1-937434-01-4

Table of Contents

Foreword

A couple years ago, I created a presentation intended to give some insight to our newer employees on what makes Caterpillar great, and what we need to do to sustain our position as the world's leading manufacturer of construction and mining equipment, diesel and natural gas engines, industrial gas turbines and diesel-electric locomotives. I thought a lot about products. They are the most tangible thing we do. Plus, in many cases they are huge, powerful and are used to build the world. What more could you want?

But, our success is about far more than product. It is about the Caterpillar brand and all the attributes of the company that make it one of the most recognized and respected brands in the world. Our success is driven by how we present ourselves to our customers, shareholders, employees, suppliers, competitors – everyone. At Caterpillar we call that "yellow blood." It is the pride that comes with consistently delivering value – no matter what form that may take.

Product is the most obvious form of value or "content" that we deliver. It is a tangible representation of an idea, presented to the market for consumption. In a way, it is not any different than a quarterly report for investors, a competitive bulletin for a potential customer or a piece of service information for a technician. Anything that we do, anything that bears the Caterpillar design mark, says something about us. It shapes the image our consumers have about us. It drives their decision making process. It creates our success.

My particular area of responsibility lies with the creation, distribution and support of technical information needed to support customers during the lifecycle of their product. The content we deliver has an immediate and apparent impact on the value proposition for both customers and the dealers who support them. It impacts their efficiency, effectiveness, Profit & Loss statement, balance sheet and arguably most importantly, their safety.

Caterpillar has a long, rich history of exceptional product support. It is a key differentiating feature. The content of our product support is the information and the context that enables a consistent, valued customer experience. Content is a strategic asset that is foundational to that competitive advantage.

The Content Pool very effectively elevates "content" to its appropriate status – a strategic asset that should be managed with the same care and feeding as the tractors, engines or engineering blueprints that we at Caterpillar deliver. Alan provides the reader with simple, compelling logic that is highly valuable when putting together and selling the business case to improve the way we manage one of our most important assets: content.

Leslie Paulson
Manager, Technical Information Solutions
Caterpillar, Inc.

Introduction

What does your company do?

It's a simple enough question, yet in all my years of consulting I've found that it is often the hardest one to answer. Ask seven people in an organization and you will get as many different answers; sometimes you will get more as people often supply two or three definitions of what they believe a company does. And despite mandated mission statements, employee briefings, "elevator pitches," and other types of corporate messaging, I often find that the view of what a company does is very different between the shop floor and the executive suite.

The thing is, there is no wrong answer to the question "What does your company do?" Every response is a valid one. People's perceptions of what a company does are colored by what their day to day tasks are.

But if there is one response that is more prevalent than any other, it is that "we make X" or "we sell a product that does X." This is no real surprise as most enterprises are judged by the product or service that they offer – yet this is rarely what they are actually in business for.

Consider this often cited example: Let's look at a company that currently offers a range of drill bits for use in power tools. What would you say they are in business for? To make drill bits? Not really. Most businesses are started to either help solve a problem or fulfill a need in the market. A company that makes drill bits is actually based around a need to make holes. What they sell is the ability to make those holes, the drill bits are just the current technology for doing that. It may be that in the future they will manufacture a laser device or supply thermic lances. What they produce will have changed, but what they are in business to do won't. They will still help people make holes.

One side effect of such a change in technology can be that while the basic business need remains unchanged, companies that fail to adapt to a change in the way the task is achieved can easily lose a dominant market position. Consider the changes in long distance public transport infrastructure in the twentieth century. The need to move people across long distances was always there, but companies that built a business around the idea of being a railroad faltered, while airlines that positioned themselves as first and foremost being in the transport business, prospered.

A friend of mine who is the chief financial officer of a cable TV company in the UK, has always maintained that every company is in business to do the same thing – make a profit. See what I mean about your role in a company reflecting your opinion of what it does? But, all joking aside, I believe he has a valid point; but I don't believe he goes far enough in his holistic viewpoint.

I actually believe that no matter what product or service your company or organization provides, or what need it is trying to fulfill, that every one, from one-person consultancies to multinational mega-corporations, does the same five things:

1. Create something

Every company does something. They either create or improve on a product, or they develop and deliver a service. But these things don't just happen. They are often the result of extensive research and development efforts. Even if you don't have a formal R&D lab thinking up the best new mousetrap, as a business owner of any size you need to be constantly thinking about where your market is, and how you can adapt to meet the needs of your current market and hopefully move in to new ones. Development is an essential part of any company's operations.

2. Tell people about it

Once you have developed that thing that you do, it doesn't matter how great or revolutionary it is, you won't grow your company if you don't tell anyone about it. At one company I used to work for we used to joke that our new products weren't released, they just escaped. As a result revenue growth was flat. If you don't tell people about what you do, they won't be able to use your products. You need marketing.

3. Get people to buy it

If things are working well, when you start telling people about how great your mousetrap is and how it will solve their problem and make their lives better, they will want to own one, or preferably several.And of course, you would like them to keep buying newer versions of your mousetrap as you continue to develop them. This is where sales comes in. Whether you are a solo-business operator working the phones, or you have a multi-national team of highly compensated sales executives, you still need to close the deal.

4. Collect money for it

Once you have developed, marketed and sold your mousetrap, I can imagine that you would really appreciate getting paid for it. Whether you work on an instant payment retail basis or a credit-based invoicing method, you need the money to flow. Money is the oil that lubricates any enterprise. You need it to cover your expenses, pay your staff, and if you manage things correctly, hopefully you will, as my CFO friend would put it, make a profit.

5. Create content about it

Every step of the way while doing those other four things, you are also creating content about what you do. Everyone in your organizations does it. From the simplest email message, to complex policy and operation documents, to legal notices, to training courses, technical manuals, design specifications, manufacturing and servicing instructions. From websites to market collateral, sales brochures to proposal responses.The content you create about your product or service is often as essential and influential to the brand image of your company as a commercial or advertisement would be. The collateral and content that support your product or service are an important part of customer interaction, satisfaction, and overall customer experience.Content is pervasive throughout your company and essential to every aspect of your business strategy and growth.

The first four activities outlined above are usually overseen by someone with executive level (CXO or VP) authority, yet content creation is ignored as a core strategic activity – why?

The Content Pool

The first step to answering that question is to consider what we mean by "content"?

Dictionary.com[2][1] offers 11 different definitions of the word "content," but the ones that concern us here are:

con·tent

[kon-tent] **– noun**

1. *something that is to be expressed through some medium, as speech, writing, or any of various arts.*
2. *substantive information or creative material viewed in contrast to its actual or potential manner of presentation.*

---

[1] http://dictionary.reference.com/browse/content

Much has been written over the last twenty or so years on how we are now drowning in a sea of information. More information is being produced now than at any other time in human history. Information is all around us and is available to us in ways that just a few decades ago would have seemed like the wild imaginings of a science fiction writer. In many ways we take it for granted, but it is amazing that most of us can access almost unlimited resources of human knowledge and information with just a few button clicks or by running our fingers over a touch screen. We are becoming used to having vast amounts of information available and having the answer to any question be resolved almost immediately. We are all creating information, and content, every time we interact online.

I have often heard the lament that "no one writes any more." The fact is that we are writing more than we ever have, it's just that the medium and mechanism has changed from pen and paper to bits and networks. The explosive growth of social networks and the switch to texting as a primary source of communication have changed the landscape. With such changes in everyday life comes an expectation that the equivalent model also exists in the business world.

The lines between home and work are blurring, a shift that is also driven by the increase in virtual teams and the work anywhere mobile workforce; particularly in knowledge based industries where physical co-location may not be necessary and more people are transitioning away from the traditional office environment.

While we all have access to this sea of information, within a particular organization we need to contribute, collaborate, and have access to a set of information that is relevant to that organization. We all create, as well as consume, a collection of information that I refer to as "The Content Pool."

Why the Content Pool is important

Your content is where all your company's intellectual property resides. Everything about your company, the products you produce, the way you operate and your plans for the future are captured in the content you produce as an everyday activity. From the simplest email, to internal policies and procedures, to technical manuals, marketing collateral, and websites, it's all valuable information. And don't forget your customers are also creating information about the way you and your products work (or don't) on social networks, online forums, and various other collaborative venues. All that content is useful and needs to be identified, captured, and managed.

The cliche that "everyone is replaceable" is something of a truism, but it doesn't apply to your content. Your content will outlast even the most loyal employees, but if you don't realize that those same employees are also creating and contributing to The Content Pool, then you can lose significant amounts of institutional memory, with severe impact on your business.

During the summer of 2009 my wife and I took a trip to the New Mexico Space Museum. While I was there I got chatting with one of the museum volunteers who had worked in the astronauts' office during the Apollo days. During the conversation he offered the observation that:

> There were things they did back then that we can't do today.

This reminded me of a conversation I'd had many years ago while visiting one of the NASA facilities where an engineer had told me that even though the Saturn V rockets on display at the Cape

Kennedy launch site in Florida and the Johnson Space Center in Houston, TX were fully functional, they could never be put back into service as no one knows how to operate them. As the engineers from the Apollo projects dispersed or died off, and the focus shifted to Shuttle operations, the institutional knowledge needed to launch a Saturn V disappeared.[2]

Recounting this story a few days later prompted another memory. Several years ago, the consulting company I was working for was engaged to help identify just such a loss of institutional knowledge. During our time at the company we discovered that a tradition had developed among the people who worked on the assembly line to keep a small notebook in their overalls pocket. These notebooks were used to write down workaround steps or take notes on how to improve the efficiency of the assembly process. Many of the notebooks had photocopies of pages from the company's official assembly manuals pasted in with notations added.

We also found out that the people with the longest service could assemble the product in about half the time the official process said it would take. The increase in efficiency was due to a combination of experience and the tricks and short cuts they had written in those notebooks.

The real problem came when the longest serving employees retired or moved on and took their notebooks with them. The institutional knowledge was lost. Each new person employed on the assembly process would start from zero with the official procedures and have to relearn all the tricks that their predecessor had developed.

---

[2] This story is an extract from a post I wrote on The Content Pool blog (http://-4jsgroup.blogspot.com/2009_07_01_archive.html)

Because the existence of the notebooks was never officially acknowledged, they were never included in any part of the company's knowledge capture procedures. Our recommendation was to engage the people in the company who had the best skills for interviewing subject matter experts – the technical documentation group. From that point on a monthly review session was held where a technical writer would sit down with the assembly team and take notes on what the engineers had written down in their personal notebooks over the previous four weeks.

When someone is leaving the company, for whatever reason, don't just conduct an exit interview with the HR department, do a proper debrief and capture not only their notes, but the inherent knowledge and process tricks that are in their heads too.

> If NASA had done this, we might still be able to fly the Saturn V.

What I am advocating in the pages of this book is that to be truly effective we need to take a more holistic view. In fact, as I propose in the summary section, I believe that most organizations need a CCO – a Chief Content Officer.

Corporate knowledge is not all about flying space ships, building engines, erecting buildings, or designing software. Every scrap of content can be a valuable and essential part of the way your company operates. Even a simple email message may contain a critical piece of operational information, or a set of meeting notes can lead to a new way of doing things or create a new market opportunity. To be truly effective, that information needs to be shared in such a way that others can contribute, collaborate, and build on the idea.

Content of all sorts is vital to all aspects of a company's life; without it none of the other four strategic activities I outlined earlier – development, marketing, sales, and finance – could operate.

Earlier, I asked why content creation is often overlooked as a strategic activity, I believe that, unlike the other core activities, it isn't seen as a specialist activity. Because everyone does it, no one manages it, and no one is accountable.

This book is about how to change that. Reading this book will help you to identify, organize, manage and leverage your company's largest hidden asset – its content.

Identifying Your Content

1

Why Is Content So Important?

Early in my career, I managed the technical publications department at a large aerospace manufacturing facility. During one budget meeting a senior executive said to me "I don't see why we need to be paying for these writers. Anyone can write, and all you do is produce brochures. My secretary could do that."

My answer to that challenge was to pass over a sheaf of engineering drawings and ask if he would be comfortable flying on an aircraft where the repair procedures were based on his secretary's interpretation of the engineering drawings. This was no slight at his secretary, who was in fact one of the best and most efficient I've ever come across. I was making a point not just about the production of content, but also the quality, and perhaps most importantly, the risk associated with it.

In the introduction, I talked about how your content is the one place where all your company's intellectual property resides – a point I will return to later in the book – and that the institutional knowledge inherent in your content can outlive even the most long-tenured employees. Your content is the life blood that is continually circulating around your organization.

But another aspect of your content is just as important: its quality. If your blood turns anemic, then your overall health suffers; if the quality of your content drops, then your company suffers. Bad content can cost you lost business or even have legal implications. It's even possible that poor content can mean senior company officers go to jail.

Content strategy and content management are a vital part of any operational risk assessment and are all too often overlooked.

Here are a few examples of how bad content can affect a company:

- The British National Health Service is reported as spending up to £86m a year on thousands of websites that are difficult to find, badly designed, and irrelevant to patient needs, according to a leaked government report.[1]

- At the 2011 Field Service conference, I heard the story of how poor service information resulted in one company spending $100,000 just to fix a single screw.

- The BBC reported on a study that claims simple spelling errors on websites could cost millions in lost sales.[2]

- and so on –there will be plenty more examples of the impact of bad content as we progress through the book.

Content strategist Scott Abel puts it succinctly when he says:

> As a content management strategist, I've helped clean up some pretty big content messes. Almost all of these content cleanups were motivated by business disasters such as lawsuits, regulatory action, public relations nightmares ... you get the picture. All of these expensive content woes could have been avoided if the organizations involved had realized one important fact:
>
> **Content is a business asset worthy of being managed efficiently and effectively.**

[1] http://www.guardian.co.uk/society/2010/aug/04/nhs-websites-failing-patients

[2] http://www.bbc.co.uk/news/education-14130854

> That's right, content – words, images, multi-media, and all the other so-called creative work that goes into fueling an organization – should be managed just like the parts in a manufacturing plant or the dollars in an investment portfolio.[3]

Some companies are aware of their content and have some content policies and practices, but unless they treat their content in a holistic, strategic manner, such efforts can lead to information silos. Often effort is duplicated or becomes inconsistent, out of date, and frankly useless.

Companies are becoming increasingly awareness that as they extend their markets and territories, often into a global environment, the information associated with their products and services should not only be current, but should be available anywhere and at anytime a customer or partner needs it. The Internet has created an expectation of "always on" and "always available," and good content is the key to meeting that expectation.

This is particularly important for producers of manufactured goods and equipment, where support is now expected to be available in the field, the factory, and the call center, as well as accessible via home computers and mobile devices. Anyone dealing with service and support information, at any location, needs to be getting the right information, from a single trusted source, at the same time. And, that information needs to be current and available throughout the product's life cycle.

---

[3] "Controlling Authors, Enforcing Content Creation Rules, and Effectively Managing Terminology No Longer An Option" http://thecontentwrangler.com/-2011/01/31/controlling-authors-enforcing-content-creation-rules-and-effectively-managing-terminology-no-longer-an-option/

Content lifecycle management is just as important as, and is an integral part of, product lifecycle management and should be treated as such. Whether your product is gears, bits and bytes, dollars, or billable hours, you should be aware of both how it changes over time and how you produce and manage the content that reflects those changes.

Stale information

The sad truth is that I have seen estimates in various presentations that claim that as much as 90% of information published by companies is stale. In an article on IT Business Edge,[4] writer Michael Vizard gives an excellent example of why information becomes stale: "The problem with product documentation these days is that while tons of time and effort go into creating it, once it's up on the website, most companies forget about it."

While he is focused on product documentation, the same story could easily be applied to many different types of content where publishing is seen as the last part of the creation process, and no thought is given to maintaining it.

Vizard also points out content is all too often disconnected from "any meaningful business process." The net effect of disconnecting content from the business process is that it does not get updated when things change. The result is the stagnation of the content and an exponential decrease in its usefulness to both the business and the customer. This leads to a lack of confidence in content that should, in fact, be the authoritative source.

---

[4] http://www.itbusinessedge.com/cm/blogs/vizard/a-little-product-documentation-help-please/?cs=47966

Content creation inefficiency

There is a corresponding lack of efficiency in the actual process of content creation. Some estimates claim that without proper management and control, up to 75% of the traditional content creation process is wasted effort. While individual inefficiencies and mistakes may at first sight seem small, they can soon add up. In fact, one study suggests that fixing bad writing and content errors costs US industry as much as $3.1 Billion a year.[5]

So, how do you avoid such costly mistakes?

The rest of this book presents a methodology that will enable you to make the most of your content, not only preventing unnecessary costs, but also preparing and positioning your content to help reduce internal costs and generate more revenue. Your content should add to your bottom line, not detract from it.

The methodology is broken down into four stages:

1. Identifying your content.
2. Organizing your content.
3. Managing your content.
4. Leveraging your content.

Within each part we present a mix of practical examples, ideas, and concepts that will you develop an effective, holistic content strategy.

---

[5] http://boston.com/news/education/higher/articles/2010/05/19/failure_to_communicate/

2

What Do You Produce Now and How Do You Use It?

In the introduction I talked about how everybody in an organization produces content. Some of it may be produced as part of a formal process, but the majority of it is most likely created informally on an ad-hoc basis as part of doing different tasks. In fact, it is likely that most people do not even realize that they are creating strategic assets as part of their regular jobs. So it is perhaps inevitable that the content produced goes unrecognized and unmanaged.

So how do you go about changing that?

It's a well known maxim that in order to manage anything the first thing to do is quantify it and build an accurate picture of what it is you are trying to manage. In other words, if we want to make something better, we need to know what we are doing now, and in this particular case, how much content we are producing as an organization, what it costs to produce that content, and what it is being used for.

So, if content creation is happening all across the organization, how exactly do you measure it?

The next three chapters are aimed at helping you identify and quantify the content in your organization.

To start on the journey of transforming all the content you produce into a measurable, manageable, strategic asset, you first need to answer three questions:

- What content do you produce now,
- How do you use that content
- What does it cost to produce and distribute?

What content do you produce now?

Trying to answer this question may at first seem like a daunting task, but if approached systematically, it can be done efficiently.

If you do a web search for the term "content audit" you will come across two distinct types of audit:

- An assessment of a website in preparation for a redesign or the introduction of a website management tool.

- An assessment of all content in an organization as the basis for a unified content strategy.

While the first is perhaps the most common, it is the second category that this book addresses.

A content audit should be one of the first things you do as part of any content strategy exercise. It isn't a fun exercise, and it will be labor intensive, but the results will provide a solid foundation for everything that comes afterwards.

In the ideal content audit you should examine every piece of content as thoroughly as possible, making notes on its various attributes, its place in the business process, where it's stored, how it's distributed, its audience, etc. Of course, examining every piece of content is most likely to be impractical, so it is fine to select a representative sample for each content type.

Prepare a check list or survey and use this as a basis for logging all the various content types and activities that you come across when conducting the audit.

You also need to define what you mean by "content" and the scope of what will be included in the audit. How far do you intend to go in diving into your own organization's content pool? In theory you could include every scrap of content and information produced, from the annual report to the post-it notes stuck on your engineers' computer monitors. In practice, I would recommend starting with any official company-produced documents (whether they are used internally or externally) and associated media such as engineering drawings, videos, graphics, etc.

One point you need to consider while conducting such an audit is that a large proportion of company documents tend to be stored as e-mail attachments. During the few years I worked in the disaster recovery business we estimated that as much as 60% of our clients corporate documents were sitting on the email server as attachments at any given time. Even when companies have central storage process and technology for building on-line libraries and sharing documents most still tend to end up as email attachments.[1]

During a content audit, I would also recommend that you engage a third-party content strategist to assist with, and guide, the process. A third-party will look at your content with a fresh pair of eyes, free from assumptions and inherited knowledge. They can also ensure that the audit stays focused and in scope.

You will probably find that the majority of the content you produce falls into one or more of the following categories; and it may be advisable to select a subset of these as a starting point:

---

[1] http://distractedenterprise.com/index.php/stats-the-sharepoint-adoption-gap/

- Marketing materials
- Company Policies & Procedures
- Manufacturing & Design documents
- Support and Service documents
- Training materials
- Internal and external communications.

Working with a group – for example training, technical documentation, or marketing – that is already aware of the value of its content and monitors the production process closely, is a good way to test and fine tune your audit procedures before moving on to more nebulous areas of content creation.

When conducting an audit of departments or areas of the organization that produce content, don't just look at the deliverables, but also look to see what content is created to support that activity, such as internal style guides, functional specs, etc. These can be just as important to the business process as the main deliverables, and may, as we will show in later chapters, also contain information that could be leveraged as a potential revenue source.

At the time of writing, I am actively involved in a large scale project to develop a new method of content delivery for a multinational engineering company. As a first step, the consulting team identified the major content types and sources and spent several weeks interviewing subject matter experts and developing a series of reports documenting the current, or "as is," processes. During that time we discovered many different areas where the same content was used in different processes, or where different experts knew about their own processes, but had little understanding of how their processes fit into the larger overall process. But, perhaps the most common observation was about the degree of overlap between the various processes and content types. Doing the "as is" audit helped clarify areas of duplication and provided a stable base line for defining the project's road map and an ongoing content creation, management, and delivery strategy.

How do you use that content?

Perhaps just as important as discovering what content you are producing is discovering why you are producing it.

Always ask the questions "what?" and "why?"

What is in the particular document, and why do you need it? Find out what business purpose it serves. Who is the customer for a particular type of document? Is it produced just because someone asked for it at some point in the past, or does it serve a particular need. Frequency of use is also an important factor. How often is that document used? Obviously, frequent use is a good indication of a document's importance, but you also need to bear in mind that a document that is used infrequently may still be an important part of the overall business process.

As an example, in my first management position my predecessor informed me that I was required to produce a particular report about a certain aspect of my department's activities and send it to half a dozen senior executives. This I did diligently for about six months. Then due to a family medical crisis, I was absent from the office for several weeks. When I returned and waded through the various requests, memos, and messages that had accumulated during my leave, I noticed an absence of requests for that particular report. So as a test I didn't send it out the next week. Still no complaints from any of the recipients. At my next weekly status meeting I asked my immediate boss if he ever even looked at that report. He admitted he never did, but he assumed that the other five recipients needed it. Five phone calls later and we confirmed that, in fact, no one read it. In fact no-one even recalled asking for it. It seemed that at some point in the distant past one executive had asked the then incumbent departmental manager for such a report. The manager had taken it on himself to copy the other executives as a courtesy. After that, this particular report had just become part of the "way we do things" and had been handed down from manager to manager. Removing it from the content production flow had no impact on the way I managed my department or its performance. In fact, it freed up several hours a week and saved a lot of unread paper.

So you must always ask if a particular piece of content is:

- needed to help the business process,
- required for legal reasons,
- needed to help generate revenue.

If it doesn't fit one of these three categories, you should question whether it is necessary in the first place.

What does it cost to produce and distribute?

As well as knowing what you are producing, it is also vital to know how much it is costing you. I am always amazed by the apparent lack of interest in the cost of producing content. When I ask the simple question, "how much does it cost to produce this document?" in the vast majority of cases the response is "we don't know." Even from managers of departments, such as technical publishing, training, and marketing, whose prime activity is producing such content.

The easiest way to calculate cost is to track how many hours individuals contribute to the creation (or revision) of a certain set of content, then multiply that by their hourly rate, plus an amount that represents the operational overhead. The actual math isn't difficult, but figuring out the base numbers may take some work.

If you haven't already done this exercise, I can almost guarantee that the results will surprise you. Content production, especially uncontrolled and unmanaged content production, can be an expensive proposition. For instance, a recent online article[2] described how an unmanaged internal document review process was calculated as costing the company $3,500 a page!

Production costs don't only cover the cost of actual creation. You must also factor in the actual cost to translate (if applicable), publish, and deliver in all of the media you publish in (print, online, help, etc.).

And then there's distribution.

During the research phase for this book, I was having a conversation with a couple of people at a large manufacturing company about the cost of their documentation. At the start of the conversation, I was expecting to hear all about the software they used to author, manage, and publish their information, or even about the cost of training and retaining skilled technical communicators. But, the conversation quickly turned to one aspect that most of us (and I include myself in that) often completely overlook – the cost of actually getting the information into our customers' hands. This company's largest content-related cost is simply Postage!

---

[2] http://thecontentwrangler.com/2006/02/02/3500_a_page_six_degrees_of_documentation

When we talk about modern technical communications and publishing systems, processes, and technology, we tend to think about digital creation and delivery. Along with that comes an assumption that most, if not all, of our customers are in some way connected to the Internet. There is a lot of talk (and again I'm just as guilty as anyone) of web delivery, mobile delivery and the bright digital future we are all marching towards. Yet that is a very Anglo-American-centric view of the world.

Recently, someone at Facebook developed a visualization of all the various Facebook connections,[3] and the image that appeared turned out to be a startlingly accurate rendering of a map of the world, except that large areas of that map were dark. It reinforced the message that even if we are producing information digitally, we can't assume that if we are operating on a global scale everyone who needs access to our information has a wired connection,or that the speed of the connection or political climate/policies allow access to that particular site/media.

So back to my earlier conversation. The company I was talking to uses modern authoring processes, along with content management tools, to efficiently single-source their documentation into many different deliverables. But, their products are literally used all over the world, including in some of the world's most inhospitable and remote locations. Not everyone is wired, so instead they ship sets of DVDs to customers and business partners. Depending on the product being used, the DVD sets can consist of anything from 3 to 12 separate discs. And, they ship 15,000 such sets every month. While the cost of shipping a set of DVDs within the US may be relatively cheap, the cost of shipping one set of DVDs to a user working in the African jungle may be as

---

[3] http://facebook.com/notes/facebook-engineering/visualizing-friend-ships/469716398919

high as several thousand dollars. In addition to the actual postage, there is the cost of import duties, time to fill out customs forms and get approvals, on top of the actual delivery cost. I was told of one DVD set that involves the monthly rental of a boat and boatman to delivery it along a jungle river!

The total annual postage and delivery cost of DVDs for this company is millions of dollars and recent increases in postage rates have meant a disproportionate rise in that overhead. So, next time you are considering the cost of your documentation, don't just think about the investment needed to actually create the content, think about what it takes to actually get that information into the hands of all your customers, no matter where they are located.

Summary

Remember you need to establish:

- What content do you produce now,

- How do you use that content

- What does it cost to produce and distribute?

3

Identifying the Audience: Today and in the Future

So, by now you should know what content you produce, what it's for, and how much it costs you; but perhaps the larger question is, "does it actually do what you created it to do?"

The first rule of any content creation process is to know your audience. Yet the vast majority of content is created with no real analysis or knowledge of the people who will actually consume that content. Knowing your audience is key to producing useful content.

In short, you need to define your audience. Traditionally, when thinking about an audience we just tend to think about "who," as in, "Who is seeing this?" But, today you also have to think about where that audience is finding and accessing the content. And, even though you designed it to be consumed in one environment (say a web-site viewed on a computer monitor), they may be experiencing it in another (such as a mobile phone).

You need to consider the following

- Who is my intended audience?
- Who is my actual audience?
- How do they find my content?
- How do they consume the content?

Who is my intended audience?

Once you have completed the audits and estimations of the type and volume of content, as outlined in the last chapter, you will have gone a long way towards defining the purpose of your content. That exercise should give you a strong indication of what the intended audiences are for the different types of content you have.

You should document these audience types, and I would also suggest developing a persona for each, as this will become useful in further defining strategy.

A persona defines an archetypal user of a system, or in this case, consumer of content. For instance Francis the QA Expert needs to understand the inner workings of a system to test it, while Jane the cashier needs to know how to process a return, etc.

While considering your audience, you also have to consider its size and culture. Even simple email messages have an audience. Think about where those messages are going and to whom. While you may not need to manage individual messages, or even ones going to smaller groups, think about company-wide email.

One company I worked with had what I termed an underlying culture of assumption. Most internal communications were written with the assumption that everyone who received them knew how every part of the internal culture and infrastructure worked.

For instance, an invitation to a conference call would include the password code but not the dial-in number; conference rooms would be named without saying what building or facility they were located in; all times were written as Eastern Time (but not indicated as such), even though the company had employees located across every US time zone and some international ones, too.

It was a large company that was, at the time, on a fairly aggressive growth path and recruiting heavily. As a result, many new employees became frustrated and confused, missed essential meetings, and were not able to fully appreciate the relative importance and merits of various communications. But, perhaps the greatest issue was that this culture of assumption also bled over into communications with customers and business partners.

No matter what the size of the audience, you may have to tune the content for that audience.[1] The sort of assumptions mentioned above can be frustrating on a local level, but can have serious impacts when dealing with customers.

While working on a project where I needed to install a new piece of software, I received email from the vendor saying that in order for them to issue me a license for the new software they needed the "Host ID" of my Windows laptop – that was is it, a one line request with no further explanation.

Now, about 70% of my time is spent on Mac devices of various types, MacBook, iPad, iPhone. I haven't seriously played around with a Windows machine in years, but using a Windows laptop was a requirement of this project. I had forgotten how to find the Host ID. Clicking on the My Computer icon and looking at Properties, which seemed to be the logical thing to do, was no help at all. So I sent off a quick email asking how to find this elusive "Host ID" *"Oh, it's easy"* came the reply. *"Just open a command prompt, run the ipconfig/all command, and look for the Physical Address it returns – that's the Host ID."*

Hang on a minute – so the thing you initially asked me for isn't even called that, and you expected me to know that, plus I needed to go to the OS and remember a command line I may never have used in my life! Talk about making assumptions.

---

[1] According to a recent study, chimpanzees change their method of communication based on their audience and surroundings, so it shouldn't be difficult for us to do the same – http://www.bbc.co.uk/nature/16305600.

Okay, the end process was in fact easy – but then most things are if you know how to do them. Just because you, your engineers, and your support personnel may be comfortable working in a particular environment, don't assume that your customers are just as familiar. In this case, the support engineer assumed that I was part of a shared cultural experience, in particular a shared technical Windows one. This approach can cause problems as the reach of the audience increases, especially across regional and national frontiers, even when speaking the same language.

You would think that a communication from a US company to an English one shouldn't cause too many problems, but if the sender indulges in the American habit of using sporting metaphors, especially baseball related ones, it soon becomes meaningless. Communication across language barriers makes the problem even more acute. (Some techniques for developing content for use in a global market will be discussed in the next chapter.)

Be aware that underlying assumptions about your audience, even inadvertent ones, can in fact raise barriers and prevent the intended audience from consuming your content.

When you think about the various audiences your content serves, also think about the various areas in your organization that create that content. Are different functions independently developing content for the same audience? Are sales, marketing, engineering, and support all developing content for the customer? If so, do they all use the same terminology for your products and its functions? Are they all delivering the same message?

Who is my actual audience?

So you think you have identified your audience? I can almost guarantee that your audience is a lot larger than you think it is. Consider that content that you develop for a particular set of customers may also have value for the entire market segment. Or, that content designed for use in one business process could also be applied to several others.

You should also consider the impact and use of your content by secondary (or even tertiary and beyond) audiences. There are two types of extended audiences you need to think about:

- A group outside your primary audience that is already aware of and using your content, but that you may not be fully aware of. This is a growing trend because social networking makes it easy for members of your primary audience to blog, repost, or supply links to your content to their audiences.

- A group that could be making use of, and deriving value from, your content, but is currently unaware of it. Thinking laterally about your content and how it could be applied elsewhere can often be a good way to identify groups in this category.

Think beyond the limitations of your current delivery mechanism and packaging of your information. A friend of mine is the pop-culture and music critic for a large metropolitan newspaper. He traditionally delivers his content through both the hard-copy newspaper, which has a limited circulation in one particular city, and on the paper's website, where the audience has the potential to be wider, but is generally accessed by people who are aware of the newspaper's existence. Over lunch one day we were talking about my experiences from publishing my book about the early days of the Beatles, *Before They Were Beatles*[13], as an eBook on the Kindle, and how that had become a self-sustaining seller. A few weeks later he told me how that conversation had prompted an idea on how he could open up his content to new audiences. The paper had an archive that included many early reports and reviews of various musicians who got their start in the city. By repackaging these as an eBook he could now reach out to fans of those particular artists, who would search for content by an artist's name without ever needing to know the name of the newspaper.

Another thing to consider when content goes beyond its original intended use and reaches new audiences is: how do you manage this? How do you control what gets exposed to whom, and at what point in the business process? There's a tradeoff between the value of having information out there and the danger of losing control over that information. So you need to be aware of that fact and consider what content you want to control and what you are happy with being propagated. But bear in mind that the more information you have out there, the more potential reach you have into new audiences and new markets.

You also need to be aware that your audience is evolving. The audience you have today isn't the same as yesterday's audience and will be different from tomorrow's audience. They may need the same content to achieve the same results, but expectations of how they find and interact with the content changes as technology and cultural norms shift.

How do they find my content?

When I started as a content developer in the aerospace industry most of my research was done based on paper engineering drawings and microfilmed archives. Today I would expect to find that same information delivered as 3-dimensional computer-aided design files and Internet search engine results. In some companies I have worked with in recent months, they even have virtual reality labs.

That sounds fine for a high tech manufacturing world like aerospace, but even some of the simplest content development environments have undergone drastic changes and so have the expectations of those using them. Consider, for instance, a high-school history report.

I often tell the story of how this was bought home to me by watching my youngest daughter approach compiling the information for a high-school US History report on Pearl Harbor. To research her project, the first thing she did was go to Google, search for "Pearl Harbor," and start visiting links. Her first stop was Wikipedia.

Then she got on Facebook and YahooIM and started using messaging to ask friends who were online for recommendations. These friends were literally from all around the world, including a family friend in Japan, so she was given access to resources that gave totally different perspectives from those given in the classroom and local school board-approved text books.

As I watched, she soon had six different windows open on her iMac and was pulling information from multiple sources into her own document, interactively building the structure and narrative as she went. One friend suggested going to a social bookmarking site and searching using a variety of user-applied tags. Instead of being driven by a pre-defined taxonomy she was now applying a community-derived folksonomy.

Of course, being a bibliophile and a bit of a history geek, I had a few good old-fashioned print books on World War II sitting in my home office. I proudly placed them on the edge of my daughter's desk and suggested she look through them for information on Pearl Harbor, too. She dutifully picked up a couple of the books and started flicking pages over, skimming through the contents. "Why don't you use the Table of Contents or Index?" I asked. "That just confuses me. I can find stuff quicker this way," she replied, looking in bemusement at her obviously aged father. I sat back and watched her navigate the books for a few minutes. She quickly found what she needed – and then I realized what she was doing. She was "browsing" just as if she was online.

That's when I started to question the paradigm that has informed the way I've thought about content delivery for over two decades. The book-driven, structured document paradigm may have been ideal for my generation, but what about the new generation?

Since that moment of realization, I have continued to watch and learn how people use today's technology to access information and tried to extrapolate from that what they will expect in the not too distant future.

For kids raised as part of the digital generation, the first place they go to find information is the Internet and social networks. Over the last few decades we have moved from a traditional broadcast model to a more personal mode of content delivery, and audience expectation has changed along with it.

The traditional model was that we would produce our content and then push it out to a pre-defined location, like a central library of printed manuals, or even a bunch of PDF files on a website, and expect that our audience would:

- Know where this central depository was located,
- Know how to access that central depository,
- Know how to navigate through it to find what they needed.

These repositories of information would also:

- Try to include everything that we thought the intended audience would need to use our products the way that we designed them.

- Include an imposed taxonomy that we decided was the best way to organize and structure the content.

These assumptions (there's that word again) worked well for centuries while the primary medium and distribution method was paper, but as illustrated above, the primary method used by people today to find content is the simple search. Search has replaced index cards, libraries, tables of contents, and indexes. It has also removed the need for any knowledge of how the content is stored and organized.

Today's preferred model is "give me just the information I want, at the time I need it, and in the format and on the device I prefer." You need to be designing content that is flexible enough to satisfy both your traditional audience and the new paradigm. You should also watch trends and cultural shifts and position your content to be usable in future environments if possible.

For instance, at the time of writing, YouTube is the second most popular search engine on the Internet behind Google. The transfer of information and content is moving away from text to a more visual representation. Are you prepared to design, develop, and deliver your content as the animations, video, or maybe augmented reality that tomorrow's audiences may be demanding?

Even if you aren't preparing your content to be consumed this way, it can still end up being delivered through channels you haven't designed it for. I was told of one engineering company that discovered there were YouTube videos showing someone navigating through their paper documentation, in such a way that the print information was clearly visible.

But this shift isn't only about the next generation. Social media marketing guru and author Gary Vaynerchuck[2] claims that our grandparents are better positioned to deal with the changing model of interactions than we are. His point is that the "push" broadcast culture is being rapidly replaced by one based on social interaction that in many ways resembles the way small town social and economies used to work, the difference being that most of that interaction is now digital rather than in person, and the potential catchment area is now global. This observation is perhaps supported by the fact that the fastest growing demographic on sites such as Facebook is in the 55+ plus age range.[3]

In short, to reach multiple developing audiences you shouldn't lock your content into a single format of media. I was listening to a podcast[4] recently about a massive history research project that the BBC undertook in the 1980s. For its time it was a technologically advanced project, but they bet the future on laser-discs and hardcoded all the content so it could only be stored and read on laser-discs. No format-neutral versions were kept. As a result, all that research data was inaccessible to the vast majority of the British public, its intended audience, for over twenty years. And it took over 5 years to unlock the data and get it into a format where it is now available on the web.

---

[2] http://garyvaynerchuk.com/

[3] Facebook experienced a staggering 922.7% growth between 2009 and 2010 for users aged 55+ – http://www.istrategylabs.com/2010/01/facebook-demographics-and-statistics-report-2010-145-growth-in-1-year/

[4] Yet another relatively new content delivery mechanism that business hasn't even scratched the surface of yet in terms of its potential to reach new customers.

When talking about audiences we tend to think about the people who consume the content we produce, but in many instances you also need to consider your own organization as an audience. Most companies have suppliers who deliver content. The larger the company or organization, the incrementally larger the number of suppliers. You need to consider:

- Do your content development policies and procedures developed internally also apply to your vendor suppliers?

- How about when you work with partner companies?

- How well are you organized to accept, interpret, and maybe even integrate someone else's content?

If you are large enough organization, it may be possible to require your suppliers to follow your content development and delivery standards (See Chapter 9 for more on standards). If that isn't possible, then maybe you can agree to use an existing industry standard for content exchange. As a minimum, asking for content in a format-neutral model will make receipt and integration of that information into your content development process a lot easier.

As I discussed above, there may be a significant difference between the way you designed and expected content to be found and the way that your audience actually finds it.

I was having a discussion recently with a company that was looking at taking some content they traditionally deliver in print and delivering it online. The documentation specialist I was talking with insisted there should be a hierarchically structured table of contents, because he thought that is how customers find their way around the information. Yet, while this may have been true for the print version, studies of user behavior for some of the company's other online documentation showed that the majority of customers use the simple search function and that tables of contents are hardly ever used. The accepted navigation techniques for one medium do not necessarily carry over into another one, even for the same content.

The key is to make your content findable.

Findability is more complex than just making it searchable. Search Engine Optimization (SEO) of content has grown to be a high profile marketing technique for web-site content, as people develop practices that "guarantee" to move your web pages higher up search engine results. In many ways this is a beneficial tactic, but beware that overuse of SEO techniques and an over reliance of keywords can render your content unusable, with more search keywords than quality content. At the end of the day quality content will generate web traffic. SEO should be used as an additional tactic, not as a strategy for making content findable.

Findability comes from things such as:

- Well-designed navigation links
- Clear labeling
- Color coding
- Content that is relevant to context
- Clear organization
- Consistent navigation

Perhaps the one thing above all that drives findability is quality, useful content. This will get your information passed around.

The one thing that hasn't changed with the development of the digital world, is that the strongest recommendations come from your peers. Word of mouth is still the most effective form of advertising, and the whole social network phenomenon is based on this concept.

If you provide quality content that is useful, then people will pass it around. Peer networks are the most trusted source of information (and unfortunately sometimes, disinformation). Social networks make it easier than ever for these sort of recommendations to be propagated through blog posts, link sharing, etc.

One technique to make your content findable is to make sure that, instead of telling people what you do, you create content that answers questions about how you can help them. Going back to the earlier example of the company that manufactures drill bits, the obvious strategy would be to create a catalog of the various sizes of drill bits with the expectation that people will select, and hopefully purchase, the bits they need.

Consider instead if they created content that answered questions like "How do I make a ½ inch hole in a breeze block wall?" Then, in addition to providing a how-to response that might get shared, they could also link to the correct selection of bits to use and maybe also up-sell associated equipment, which might come from a business partner, but for which they get a referral fee.

Most people look for content not to know "what" something is, but to answer "how do I...?"

How do they consume content?

A vital part of your content strategy is considering how your audience actually interacts with your content and what devices and media they use to consume and use that content. This is easier to do today than at any previous time. It's as simple as listening. There are a variety of tools available that allow you to both listen to and engage in conversation with your audience about your content. Set up searches for your company name, products, industries you serve, or even the names of some of your more vocal customers (champions and detractors alike). Use things like RSS feeds, Twitter, social networks, etc. Follow industry analysts, listen in on forums, users groups, etc. Build listening time into your content development strategy. Invest the time to listen and you can gain a distinct competitive advantage.

Listening will also give you an opportunity to see what sort of impression your company or organization makes. Are you on message? By the way, listening can mean just that. Try calling your own company office or help line periodically and see what the customer experience is like. Yes, even corporate voice mail messages should be part of your content strategy. It's all an opportunity to communicate with your customers and business partners.

Don't forget to track the multiple ways that content is presented outside the organization to investors, customers, partners, prospects, and even your competitors.

When I started as a content developer I created documents on a paper; they were then typed up into single sheets of camera ready copy and printed using traditional methods to produce paper manuals. As I mentioned earlier, my source content came in the form of engineering drawings, microfilm, and on rare occasions a computer terminal hooked up to a corporate information mainframe. Communication within the company or with customers and business partners was done through typed memos, phone, letters ,and if urgent, telex and fax. (Wow, sounds like the stone age doesn't it, but I'm only talking about the mid 1980s, a mere thirty years ago.)

Today I use multiple types of editing tools – depending on the type of content – from standard office word processors, to structured editing tools for technical documentation, to wikis (this book was written on a wiki), to website development tools, as well as graphics, animation, and video tools. My sources are invariably electronic and often come over the Internet. Being instantly connected to the largest repository of human knowledge would have seemed like science fiction thirty years ago. Today it's a part of everyday life for those of us who have an Internet connection. The content I produce is consumed online, on eReaders, laptop computers, tablet computers, mobile phones, and, yes, even print. I have no control over how it is consumed, and I have no idea which of these many options you are currently using to read this book.

In situations like this we need to design our content so it isn't constrained by the ways that people consume it, and make sure we don't include meaningless references or navigation aids. This book will be produced electronically as well as in print, so referring to page numbers would be superfluous.

A great example of ignoring shifts in the way content is consumed is network TV. At the time of writing (mid-2011), many networks still advertise upcoming shows as being on tomorrow or make a point of which particular day a show is broadcast. However, many people now time delay when they watch TV, using digital video recorders (DVRs) or similar devices. In fact, this is a practice that has been steadily growing since the introduction of the home video tape recorder in the late 1980s. My point is that such time-based information is largely irrelevant to a large section of the audience. Most search for and set up their DVRs based on the show's title, then set and forget it, with no interest in when it actually airs. The move to watching complete runs of TV shows via streaming services over the Internet, something I certainly do more of now, also changes the content delivery landscape.

When you are considering the way people consume your content, apply a little lateral thinking and you may find ways to package content around new media in a way that will open up new audiences. Consider the rise of vinyl LP albums in the sixties and seventies, and to some extent their resurgence in recent years.

> Ultimately the attribute that sealed the success of the LP in the popular market had little to do with its expanded capacity or its improved sound quality. ... LPs were the first records to be sold in foot-square cardboard jackets faced with glossy cover art which served as an alluring advertisement for the music within. This allowed them to be prominently displayed in racks or bins in virtually any kind of store; ... The LP cover became a companion piece to the listening experience by providing photographs, biographical information and promotional copy.
> —Jonathan Gould, *Can't Buy Me Love: The Beatles, Britain and America*[5]

The key to having a flexible content strategy is to think about future proofing. The world is changing, and the way you design, develop, create, and distribute your content needs to be positioned to take account of that. As discussed above, don't lock your content into formats or media. Use standards-based content development practices that are format independent. Separate content from format and don't recreate content for different media; that can be handled by software and automation. Create once, use many times – commonly known a single-sourcing. I will cover this in more detail in Chapter 10.

With all this talk of the future and new media, don't forget about your legacy information and your older, or disconnected, audience. Paper is still the default for the vast majority of people in the world. It is still the best user interface and delivery mechanism ever created.

4

What About the Language You Use?

Every day we all see poor use of language on signs in stores and in documents. In fact, we often make a game of it, because pointing out others' mistakes is kind of fun. But, how does your business stack up? Even the simplest communications can be misinterpreted. Here are a few examples:

The sign in the parking lot outside my wife's office reads:

**NO PARKING
VIOLATORS
WILL BE
CHARGED**

The lack of punctuation changes the intended meaning.

Or, a tire store I drive past regularly has this sign:

IF IT'S IN STOCK,
WE'VE GOT IT

No mistake over the meaning, in fact it's stating the obvious – so what was the point of the message?

Or a sign above a convenience store aisle:

BABY NEEDS
ALCOHOL

This last one is not just a poor juxtaposition of language, you have to wonder about the actual product placement in the store.

These examples may be a bit of fun, but language mishaps can be costly. In fact, they can be fatal. Back in my aerospace days the phrase "Cut the electrical power" in a service manual was taken literally by one technician (whose native language wasn't English). Instead of turning the power off (which was the instruction's intent), he took a pair of shears and sliced through the aircraft's electrical circuit killing himself.

Even when everyone speaks the same language, ambiguity can still cause problems. Consider the following incident: the tower at an airport in a country with a history of severe weather issued a command to "clear the runway." Most of the vehicles around the runway moved away from the area, but to the driver of the snowplow this was the command to do his job and, he thought, remove accumulated snow from the runway. He drove onto the runway and only narrowly avoided a collision with a landing aircraft.

Liability and language

What about the language you use? Is it costing you money or even making you legally liable?

The following is a hypothetical scenario I sometimes use when discussing this issue at conferences and with clients, and while it may present an extreme case, it is based on real life examples.

"Karl" is the CEO and owner of a 100 person software company that is experiencing rapid growth in both domestic and overseas markets. In fact, domestically his sales team has identified a new vertical market and is going after it aggressively and making significant wins. This should be all good news.

However, Karl has a language problem. The content his company is producing is costing him money:

- They have localization and translation issues
- Customer service is flooded with calls
- and they are facing a possible law suit

All because of the language they used.

Localization

Legislation in new global markets means that they now have to deliver the user documentation in local languages and have the product's user interface also display in the local language. The need for translating has gone from one or two additional languages to over twenty. Translation costs are also affected by the fact that the existing documentation is full of jargon and buzz words that, while understood in their traditional markets, are meaningless to new industries and countries.

Customer service

In addition to the confusing jargon, the documentation uses different words for the same thing, is inconsistent, and is written from an engineer's perspective rather than a customer's, which means even more frustrated users. In fact, over 50% of the support calls can be answered with information that is already in the documents, but customers can't find it, or if they can, they can't relate it to their own particular issue. As sales go up, support costs, through both official and unofficial channels, are rocketing.

Legal action

What Karl and his team didn't realize when they entered the new vertical market was that the name of one of their products potentially infringed the copyright of a much larger corporation that was already entrenched in that vertical. Karl's company was hit with a "cease and desist" order that could cut off a new potentially lucrative revenue stream.

It would seem that the quickest and easiest thing to do would be to change the name of the product, except the product name was written into the product code. Karl is now faced with the choice of contesting an expensive lawsuit, rewriting the underlying code for a product, or killing a product that opened a new market.

As bad as Karl's problems are, consider the legal consequences of the "cut the electrical power" instruction mentioned earlier. Here are some other examples of serious problems that had their roots in language:

- A power transformer company was sued for $5M after a transformer blew up due to badly worded and confusing documentation.

- The largest single problem area for Google in internationalizing their service was language / translation issues – accounted for 35% of all reported issues.

- EMC estimates it was spending $762,000 on internationalization errors in just one product set.

- Failure to convert English measures to metric values caused the loss of the Mars Climate Orbiter, a spacecraft that smashed into the planet instead of reaching a safe orbit.

- An FAA survey of aircraft technicians revealed that, although user evaluations of the accuracy and quality of technical manuals are generally good, the manuals themselves were noted as having poor usability.

- Using the wrong word in an accounting system cost the New York City Department of Education $1.4M.

- A badly worded sentence in a contract cost a Canadian utility company $2.3M.

- 12% of all IT projects fail because of ambiguous wording in requirements documentation.[1]

How does it happen?

It seems inconceivable that things like this happen, but in fact, they illustrate what happens when content creation and strategy goes unmanaged. The fact that we use our native language everyday means we develop a degree of familiarity, and in-built complacency, that we would not tolerate in most other areas of business.

Imagine the reactions of shareholders if a major corporation handled its money as casually as it handles the language it uses?

To resolve these issues we need to understand why they occur in the first place. While the underlying issues may be a natural complacency and cultural assumptions, the main areas of language misuse fall into one of these three categories:

---

[1] http://www.scs.carleton.ca/~beau/PM/Standish-Report.html (Standish Group's CHAOS report)

- Mistranslations / Cultural errors
- Ambiguity
- Low quality and/or rushed content development

Mistranslations

English is a very complex language; it is very difficult to use it precisely. One of the great strengths of English is its flexibility and descriptive power. Unfortunately, from a translation perspective, this is also one of its greatest disadvantages.

The situation is perfectly summarized by the following statement by Richard H. Wojcik & James E. Hoard of Boeing[27].

> Natural language permits an enormous amount of expressive variation. Writers, especially technical writers, tend to develop special vocabularies (jargon), styles, and grammatical constructions. Technical language becomes opaque not just to ordinary readers, but to experts as well. The problem becomes particularly acute when such text is translated into another language, since the translator may not even be an expert in the technical domain.

The most effective and accurate translations occur when translating from a word with a single, well-defined meaning and use. But the English habit of using the same word for many different things adds another layer of complication.

Even some of the simplest looking words in the English language can have literally hundreds of meanings depending on context. For instance, according to the Oxford English Dictionary[23]:

- The word "SET" has 446 definitions
- "RUN" has 396 definitions
- "GO" has 368 definitions
- "TAKE" has 343 definitions
- "STAND" has 334 definitions

Do you know which one to use when?

Cultural errors

According to Leslie Dunton-Downer in *The English Is Coming!*[3].

> English has fast become the number one language for everything from business and science, diplomacy and education, entertainment and environmentalism to socializing and beyond – virtually every human activity unfolding on a global scale. Worldwide, nonnative speakers of English now outnumber native speakers three to one, and in China alone more people use English than in the United States.

So if that's the case, why not just write everything in English, even with its inherent difficulties. From the trends quoted above, it seems that there is a fair chance that there will always be someone around who speaks English. However, for a variety of reasons this is a bad assumption on which to base business decisions:

- You can't control the locale and culture where your content is consumed; the person who needs it the most might be the one person who doesn't speak English.

On a personal note, I recall a business trip to visit a trade show in Amsterdam, where a colleague and I managed to get ourselves lost in the maze of city streets. "No problem," we thought, "everyone here speaks English." Of course, none of the three people we stopped and asked for directions could speak English. French or German, yes – but not a word of English. In fact it was a conversation in broken French that eventually helped us reach our destination.

- While English may be the ascendent language in some parts of the world, in others it is declining, and other languages, notably Spanish, are on the increase.

- Delivering content in the local language will be better received and give you a competitive advantage. Even in a global market place, people still want to feel that you understand and care about their local culture.

Cultural issues can also affect the use of English among native speakers. Many books, and probably almost as many stand-up comedy routines, have been written about the differences between American English and British English; as George Bernard Shaw famously remarked, "two nations separated by a common language."[2] Add in Australia, New Zealand, Canada, etc. and you can see the potential for even more misunderstanding. But it's not just international borders that can cause issues.

---

[2] The exact source of this quote seems to be lost to the mists of time. I have seen it attributed to Winston Churchill, Oscar Wilde, George Bernard Shaw, and even Mark Twain – Shaw seems to be the most common and consistent attribution, although apparently the phrase doesn't appear in any of his writings.

I was born and spent most of my early life in a town just outside of Manchester in the Northern English county of Lancashire. The first college I went to was in the port city of Liverpool about thirty miles to the West. For my second engineering degree I went to college in the city of Bradford, forty miles to the East over the Pennine hills in the county of Yorkshire. Three cities all within a comparatively short distance of each other, yet all three with distinctly different cultures and use of language. While at Bradford I met my wife, who is from Bristol in the South West of England, yet another culture and language. And after over 15 years of living in various parts of the USA, on both East and West coasts, we now reside in Texas. So you can only imagine how mixed my linguistic repertoire is. I may still have the British accent, but I don't sound as if I'm from anywhere in particular.

I've heard similar stories about the differences between French and French Canadian, or Spanish and Mexican Spanish, etc. And of course each region, or even parts of a city, will have its own cultural tropes and references. Even within what we may think as a common language there are regional differences. For instance, within Latin American Spanish, there is a different word for "bolt" in Argentina, Peru, and Columbia. And as a friend from Montreal remarked when discussing this topic, "I won't even touch the French Canadian vs French Quebecois vs Parisien French..."

If cultural confusion can affect native speakers, then accurate translation becomes even more important.

Translated content also has findability issues all its own, particularly when using "synonyms" for findability. For example, when searching for an "Oil Pan," in the US, we may include other terms like "Belly Pan" in the labeling to increase findability for those portions of the US that use these interchangeably. These become useless in other countries because when translated, they have no relevance. Each country has its own "synonyms" or "localisms."

Even if you translate the words accurately, the meaning can still be misinterpreted and cause cultural misunderstanding or even offense. This is even more of a risk with buzzwords, jargon, and slogans. Consider the following two well known slogans:

- *"Come alive with the Pepsi Generation"* – Pepsi Corporation – In Taiwan this was translated as "Pepsi will bring your ancestors back from the dead."

- *"Finger-lickin' good"* – KFC – In China this was translated as "eat your fingers off."

Such cultural considerations also need to be applied to the use of graphics and symbols. For instance while a white dove may be a symbol of peace to us, in other cultures it can signify war. The swastika, considered in many cultures a symbol of sun worship and fertility has taken on much more sinister significance for us in the West.

Even something as simple as the use of stick figures can cause issues. In some cultures stick figures can't be used, in others you need to have equal representation of male and female figures, while in yet other cultures the female form can not be shown in any representation. The use of color can also be open to misinterpretation too. Consider our use of black for mourning and death, while in China the color white serves the same purpose.

You also need to be aware that such cultural interpretations can change over time. The Anglo-American standard of using blue to indicate a male and pink for a female was only established in the 1940s and was, in fact, a reversal of what had been accepted practice for the previous twenty years.

So how do you avoid this cultural minefield? The short answer is that it is almost impossible to completely avoid it, but by being aware of these sorts of issues you can design and develop content to be as close to multicultural as possible. You should get to know the culture of the places your content will be used, and don't assume it is OK based on your experience, test it with people who live and work in that culture. Get customer feedback and test before you roll content out to a new population.

Ambiguity

While mistranslation and cultural confusion can be at times amusing, they are for the most part frustrating and annoying. Yes they can have serious consequences, but ambiguity can kill. Remember "Cut the electrical power"?

The main problem with ambiguity is that you know what you meant when you put words or symbols down in a certain order. You may not even realize something is ambiguous until it's pointed out.

A friend of mine tells a great story of a call to the support center for a manufacturer of cable modems. The lady on the phone kept insisting she needed to speak to someone called Jack despite being told repeatedly that no-one of that name worked at the call center. Eventually someone asked her why she though this mysterious Jack worked for the company. Her response: "It says so in your manuals. I was following the instructions, and it says plug the cable into the Ethernet port and telephone jack."

Even simple statements you may think are obvious can be misinterpreted. Consider this phrase that appears in nearly every software manual:

"Please press ANY KEY to continue..."

I've looked and I've never found a key marked ANY on the keyboards of my various computers over the years. OK this may be an old joke, but it serves a serious purpose. The ambiguity is once again a symptom of cultural assumptions. When working in a particular environment we develop a mutually agreed understanding of what certain words mean in a particular context. But when we use those word constructions to anyone outside that community, they can give a very different meaning.

One technique I have found the best for testing content for ambiguity is what I've termed the "friends and family" test. Give your content to someone who has no knowledge of your products or markets and see if they can understand the points you are making. There may be technical words and phrases they don't understand, that's OK. But see if they misinterpret things that you consider to be ordinary common phrases.

Low quality

A friend recently posted a quote on her Twitter account that she heard from a software Product Manager, who stated directly and succinctly during a meeting: "If we don't get the documentation right they will hate us, no matter what else we give them."

He was correct. I can attest from personal experience, that poor quality documentation can have a major, negative, impact on your business, but not only in customer frustration, and lost sales. It can also cost a lot of money internally.

According to a 2002 article in the Managerial Auditing Journal, the knock-on cost of fixing the problems caused from poor quality documentation can be up to six times the cost of actually doing the fix itself. During a presentation at the Worldware 2010 conference, a representative from Xerox stated that fixing a localization or translation problem after a product has moved into a support or maintenance mode can have a cost impact of up to thirty times the cost of fixing it during the product development phase. These sort of multipliers can very quickly add up to very large numbers.

As mentioned, customer frustration with poor content can also mean lost revenue. A report in Manufacturing Today[3] stated that the number one error that causes loss of customers in the manufacturing industry is poor communication, of which documentation is a major part.

What's the solution?

Given all the issues picking the right words, using them correctly, and translating them, is there a way to reduce the risks associated with trying to use English as the basis for communicating in a business or technical environment?

Simply put, yes. The solution is to use a controlled language.

A controlled language provides:

- A subset of a natural language.
- Restricted vocabulary.
- Restricted grammar rules.

Controlled language is designed to:

- Reduce or eliminate ambiguity.
- Reduce complexity.
- Ease Translation.

---

[3] http://www.manufacturing-today.com

Vocabulary

How many words do you know? You may be surprised at the answer. The English language is huge, and it's growing every day. It is estimated that a new word is created every 98 minutes. According to the Global Language Monitor[4] there are over 1,000,000 different words in the English language.[5]

Nobody knows, or uses, all those words; we already use our own subsets of what's available. The mix of words we select and use on a regular basis is a function of many cultural and geographical influences, while the number of words used is often tied to educational achievement.

- A typical high school graduate may know 40,000 words.

- A University graduate will know around 75,000 words

- The average person uses the most common 2,000 words on a regular basis.[6]

No matter how many words an individual may know, most people only use 10% of their vocabulary on a day to day basis.

We already have our own individual versions of a controlled language, but each vocabulary subset is unique. To make a controlled language work it needs to be one formed by consensus within a given community.

---

[4] http://www.languagemonitor.com

[5] On the day I wrote that sentence, July 21st, 2011 the actual count was 1,009,753. When I did the final edits on this page on December 29th, 2011 the count was 1,013,913 – a growth of 4,160 words in just six months.

[6] The figures for an average vocabulary vary, and there is no clear way of defining it – some research puts the vocabulary of an average high school graduate at 60,000 words – my figure is a midrange of all the ones I came across. Anyway, the base line point is, "there sure are a lot of words out there."

Restricted vocabulary

A typical controlled language will allow around 1,000 base words, plus an allowance for technical and industry specific words. But the key to the success of any sort of controlled language is the concept that:

One Word = One Meaning

For instance, instead of the word "set" having 446 possible definitions, in a controlled language to be used by engineers it might be defined as meaning only a group of related items, for example "a set of tools."

Where you might have used the word "set" to mean something else, instead you use alternatives. For instance, instead of saying "set the control at ..." you could say "move the control to ...", or instead of "set the equipment on the bench," you could say "put the equipment on the bench."

Restricted grammar rules

While it can be argued that the greatest problem with the English Language is the sheer number words and the flexibility of their use, the grammar is not without its issues. English grammar isn't as complex as some other languages, such as German, but it is full of contradictions. *The Blue Book of Grammar and Punctuation*[22] estimates the number of grammar rules in English at close to 200.

In a controlled language there are approximately 60 rules.

None of the rules have exceptions or contradictions.

Types of controlled language

So does this mean you have to create your own controlled language from scratch to meet the needs of your organization and customers? No. There are already several controlled languages and similar initiatives in place.

You can pick an existing one and use it as is or as the basis for your own. Or, you can decide to use just some of the underlying principles of controlled language. All will produce beneficial results.

Here are some existing controlled language initiatives and standards:

- British American Scientific International Commercial. BASIC English (1936)
- PLAIN English (US Government) 1970 to date
- Caterpillar Technical English (1972) – Kodak and several other companies have also developed their own controlled languages
- Smart's Plain English Program (PEP)
- White's International Language for Serving and Maintenance (ILSAM)
- Perkins Approved Clear English (PACE)
- Controlled English Grammar *COGRAM*.
- Globish
- Simplified Technical English (STE)[7]

---

[7] The author was involved in some of the early work in developing what became the STE standard in the mid to late 1980s. Even though it was originally developed for Civil Aircraft manufacturers, it soon spread to the whole of the aerospace and defense industry; and has since been adopted by markets as diverse as automotive, pharmaceuticals, and even fast food operators.

The benefits of controlled language

No matter which controlled language you use, or even if you just apply the principles, proven benefits include:

- Reduced time to market
- Quality assurance and improvement
- Standardized way of writing
- Improved safety
- Efficient authoring
- Good customer service
- Reduced burden on your customer
- Facilitates content management
- Facilitates structured authoring
- Considerable cost savings
- Cheaper, faster and better translations

Bob Jung of Google made a statement about designing software user interfaces that I believe can be equally applied to the use of language in content design, development, and delivery:

 You have to make it easy to do the right thing and hard to do the wrong thing.
—Bob Jung, Google

Think about it, clear text with only one meaning reduces potential legal liability to almost zero.

5

The Global
Language

So far, I've been primarily talking about language as a text-based method of communication. Yet there is a perhaps even more powerful technique that has a broader multicultural appeal. A method of communicating that works on an almost subliminal level – graphics.

I have often written and spoken at various conferences on the idea of graphics as a true Global Language, or at least as close to one as I think we will ever get.

According to Internet World Stats,[1] while English is still the most popular language on the Internet (but only just – Chinese is close behind), it represents only 42% of all websites. On a global scale, English is also in decline as a spoken language. The spoken language with the largest numbers of users is Chinese. As a written language, Chinese relies not on abstract symbols (letters), but on ideograms, or pictorial representations of ideas.

In *Understanding Comics*[10], Scott McCloud, a leading theoretician on using graphics to communicate, points out:

> Pictures are received information. We need no formal education to get the message. The message is instantaneous. Writing is perceived, it takes time and specialized knowledge to decode the abstract symbols of language.

The design and thought process of delivering graphical information, especially complex technical information, is far from simple. A badly designed graphic can be as ineffective at delivering in-

---

[1] http://www.internetworldstats.com/stats7.htm

formation as text written in a foreign language. An approach to resolving this problem is through the use of symbols and icons.

In the twenty-first century, it may be that visual iconography will finally help us realize a form of universal communication.

As shown in the table below, the use of pictures as a way to communicate predates the written word by several thousand years.

Table 5.1 – Key events in early communication

Date	Event
32,000 BCE	Earliest known cave decorations
20,000 BCE	Representational cave paintings
3,500 BCE	Sumerian pictographs
3,100 BCE	Earliest Egyptian hieroglyphs
1,600 BCE	First alphabet developed
1,500 BCE	Chinese develop ideographs
800 BCE	Greeks develop alphabet with vowels
900 CE	Current writing form develops

But even after the invention of the alphabet and a written language, graphics remained the primary mode of communication to the general population, as the common literacy that we take for granted is a twentieth-century phenomenon largely confined to socially and technologically advanced nations.

More people use pictures to communicate than any other form of language, especially when trying to communicate across cultural borders. For example, the first cave paintings of 32,000 years ago are largely understandable today. This is one form of communication that does not have a "legacy" problem.

As the use of pictures has developed over the centuries, many complex ideas have come to be represented in the form of simple icons or symbols. In fact, the simpler the iconic representation, the easier it is to understand and remember. Cognitive research has shown that memory for simple pictures tends to be better than memory for words.

Representational graphics

Representational graphics are perhaps the most common form of delivering complex technical information, from the simple cutaway that shows the inner workings of a watch to maintenance information for something as complex as an aircraft.

One problem with representational graphics is that they are often crowded with too much detail, causing the essential message that is being communicated to be easily lost. As McCloud notes, "realism can make you too aware of the messenger to take any notice of the message."

When we react to an image, we need to be able to move it from the physical "outside world" into our own consciousness as a "concept" or idea. By de-emphasizing the appearance of the physical world in favor of the idea of form, a graphic can place itself in the world of concepts and, as a result, carry its message much more effectively. By emphasizing the concepts of objects over their physical appearance, much has to be omitted.

In the case of maintenance documentation, this simplification is a trend that has developed over the past few decades. Originally driven by productivity and early computer storage requirements, this move toward simpler forms has also had the effect of moving the complex technical illustration toward an iconic form that can be easily understood and used by a large audience.

Iconic abstraction

There is a famous painting by the Belgian artist René Magritte entitled "The Treachery of Images." It features a representation of a pipe with the words "Ceci n'est pas une pipe." [*This is not a pipe.*] written below it.

If you think about it you will see that it is truly not a pipe, it is a painting of a pipe. The point is that this rationale can be applied to any image where a series of lines (simple or complex) can be used to represent an object. This is the basic definition of an icon.

The *Oxford English Dictionary (OED)*[23] defines an icon as "an image analogous to the thing that it represents."

As the resemblance of the icon to the real object varies, so does the iconic content. In other words, some pictures are more iconic than others. The fewer the lines that an icon uses to describe an object, the more versions of that object it can be used to describe. If we take the progression of the human face from photograph to the familiar smiley face icon we can see how it progresses from depicting one individual to depicting anybody.

Joel Katz, quoted in Richard S. Wurman's *Information Architects*[28], wrote that "the best way to show how something works is not necessarily to show what it looks like." When an image is abstracted into an iconic form, the emphasis should not be on eliminating detail but on focusing on specific details so that the essential meaning can be amplified in a way that is not possible with representational art. Termed "iconic abstraction," this approach can be very useful for communicating complex ideas through the shared language of graphics.

Over time, we come to recognize a surprising number of icons that can be readily used to communicate information. Nigel Holme, also quoted in Wurman's *Information Architects*, has said: "Everyone has the shape of familiar icons in their minds already. The key to understanding the information is to get people to picture the graphic for themselves; they see a new piece of information in relation to something they already know. Sometimes the best infographics can be just the idea of it."

The simpler the icon, the easier it can be to remember and understand, and the more things it can be used to represent. A well-designed icon needs to use semantic rendering (e.g., color, placement) to make its meaning specific to the content.

What has been described so far covers the representation of objects through simplified graphics, or icons. While the simple mapping of items to icon is possible, it is harder and may even be impossible to describe a system of icons capable of expressing all the notions and ideas that can be expressed in words. But while ideas can be difficult to convey unambiguously graphically, certain types of icon, referred to as symbols, can be used to express ideas.

Symbolic usage

Nothing is as condensed and packed with information as an understood symbol. A reasonable explanation would require a volume of words to make clear what a symbol can evoke in a moment. A symbol can be defined, according to the OED, as "a material object used to represent something abstract." In terms of technical communication, a symbol can be considered an image used to represent concepts, ideas, or actions.

Our lives are structured around symbols, and as with popular icons, their meanings can be immediately understood. Consider the symbols for Play, Pause, Fast Forward, etc., which are immediately understood due to our familiarity with audio/video recording and playback devices over several decades, from reel-to-reel tape recorders to cassettes to CDs and MP3 players, from VCRs to DVD players to online streaming media.

When used together, symbols are a powerful way of orchestrating meaning through graphics, as with A/V controls, which allow the operation of a diverse family of products and processes through simple push buttons. However, symbols, far more than icons, depend on culture and context. Be aware of this when preparing information to be used outside of a shared environment.

Combining techniques

None of the techniques described above may be powerful enough to produce a usable business graphic when applied in isolation. To effectively produce and communicate more complex information through the use of graphics may require a combination of all three techniques.

The use of graphical elements can be very powerful in describing complex concepts, however when delivering these graphics over a medium such as the Web, there are a number of design issues that need to be considered.

Understand the user

In *Dynamics in Document Design: Creating Text for Readers*[19], document designer Karen Schriver says, "When document designers focus their energies on technological issues for organizing and displaying information without first figuring out how it will be experienced by the user, they increase the possibility of information that is disjointed and harder to understand."

In other words, the first thing that must be done in designing technical information is to understand the audience and define the end user. This is not necessarily the person who defined the project, but the actual person who will use the information.

Understanding the user is key. Research cited by Don Moyer in Wurman's *Information Architects*[28], has shown that most users have the same six basic requirements:

1. A single source of information: "Tell me everything I need to know in one place."

2. Visual information design: "Give me pictures, diagrams, and graphics without long text explanations."

3. A safety net:"Make it hard to make mistakes."

4. Landmarks and navigation: "Make it clear where I am and what I need to do next."

5. Separate novice/expert tracks: "Give me a streamlined path once I become an expert."

6. Consistency: "Keep the same information structure."

Note that the second-most voiced request is for visual information rather than text. This is where a conflict between the interests of the designer and the user can often be found; namely, in the styles and types of visual information displayed. Because of their access to computers, designers often make overly pretty graphics in millions of colors floating in 3D space against some strange ethereal backdrop. Each of these design decisions makes the information less understandable. If you are not careful, information designers can easily become more interested in the creation and delivery of technology than in the central message they are trying to communicate.

Making sense of complex technical graphics requires some knowledge. Compared to prose, graphics place fewer constraints on how users read them, allowing knowledgeable searchers to find what they are looking for quickly. Conversely, complex graphics may pose difficult problems for non-expert users. In such cases, supplementary graphics, icons, and symbols (locators, arrows, etc.) may be required.

It is also important to use standard frames of reference wherever possible, including standard ways of displaying intelligence in the graphic such as hotspot links or animation commands. When designing graphics to describe a sequence of actions for training or maintenance purposes, the sequence in which they are represented becomes crucial, as the order in which people interpret visual instructions can shape their understanding and leave them with preconceived ideas of what is being communicated. Designers must guide users through the use of space, proximity, and clarity of image.

Scott McCloud has said, "Communication is only effective when we understand the forms that communication can take." This statement best summarizes the basic message of this chapter that underlying all talk of technique or technology is the essential goal of communicating a message through an easily understood medium—graphical communication.

The focus should not be on discussions about tools and technology, but on producing information that moves across boundaries. The central focus should be on creating meaning from visual content, working with the principle that the more complex the information the simpler the visual solution needs to be.

This is encapsulated by visual information design guru Edward Tufte in *The Visual Display of Quantitative Information*[24], who states his three principles of graphical excellence as:

- Graphical excellence is the well-designed presentation of interesting data.

- Graphical excellence consists of complex ideas communicated with clarity, precision, and efficiency.

- Graphical excellence is that which gives the viewer the greatest number of ideas in the shortest time with the least ink in the smallest space.

Organizing Your Content

6

Gain Through Collaboration

By now you will have audited your content so you know what is being produced, who your audiences are, and what sort of language you are using. In the next three chapters, we take the next steps and look at how you can organize your content to both make it easier to manage and position it so you can get the most benefit. We will discuss collaboration and consistency along with ways to determine where the real "pain points" in your content creation and distribution process are.

Collaboration

The key to making your content design, development, and delivery better – that is, more relevant, higher quality, etc. – is to embrace the idea of collaboration. A culture of collaboration can have a greater positive impact on your bottom line than any technology or tool ever will. But what exactly do I mean by collaboration, and why is it such a powerful concept? The *Merriam-Webster Dictionary*[26] lists several definitions for the word collaboration; however it is the first listed, and most common usage, that is perhaps the most appropriate here.

col·lab·o·ra·tion \noun \

1. *to work jointly with others or together especially in an intellectual endeavor.*

In his book, *Wikipatterns*[9], wiki evangelist Stewart Mader suggests that, "There is a special magic that happens when people collaborate. Collaboration touches on our human nature in a way that is easily felt but not so easily explained."

I wrote extensively about collaboration in my previous XML Press book, *WIKI: Grow Your Own For Fun and Profit*[15]. In that book I told the story of how, while working on the introduction in my local coffee shop, a Beatles tune started to play over the store's sound system, reminding me of the research I did several years ago for the book I wrote on the Beatles' teenage years, *Before They Were Beatles*[13]. What I discovered was that while collaboration between a group of people can produce great results, collaboration between particular individuals can produce even more remarkable results.

The band that became The Beatles went through numerous line-up changes in the first six years of its existence, growing from schoolboy band to the best rock-and-roll band in Liverpool. Yet, it was only when Ringo Starr and producer George Martin were added to the existing mix of John Lennon, Paul McCartney, and George Harrison, that they rocketed from local boys made good to an international phenomenon that changed a generation.

The ability and desire to collaborate is fundamental to the human condition. It was through working together that early humans developed into tribes of hunter-gatherers and then built communities with shared dwellings and shared infrastructure. Without the drive to collaborate and learn from each other, we wouldn't be the dominant species on this planet.

As Mader[9] points out, collaboration is a part of human nature:

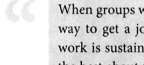
When groups work together to find the best way to get a job done, the high quality of work is sustainable because they're finding the best about themselves, combining individual complimentary strengths and talents, and refining their methods at a very high level. Because they control how they work,

> people are more self-reflective, constructively critical of their own work, and motivated to make the best contribution possible because they take greater pride in the quality of their work.

Yet among many companies there remains a reluctance to transfer this social behavior and desire to participate into the work environment. It is becoming clear that the accumulation and management of knowledge is moving away from the control of a few select individuals and towards a model where knowledge is the by-product of whichever communities an individual belongs to. The digital generation will expect to participate in, and leverage, this model, and that expectation will ultimately drive change. Companies that have already embraced the idea of community contribution are seeing the benefits and the increased efficiencies in the way they do business.

Content development silos

Within a traditional hierarchical structure it's all too easy for content silos to originate and perpetuate. Working on teams, projects, and in individual departments we become focused on our immediate tasks, and with that focus can come a lack of awareness of what other people are doing. Content is developed without asking, "is someone already doing this elsewhere?" or "does this content already exist?" and, "if I think it exists, how do I find out if it exists?"

As content strategist Rahel Anne Bailie points out, the path of least resistance often wins – it may seem easier to "just do it" than figure out how to find content elsewhere, even though doing so may have a detrimental long-term impact to the content's usability.

One of the methods I use in consulting engagements to expose this type of duplication of effort is to select a piece of information from a content set, preferably something that needs to be calculated or derived from other sources, and then track back to see how many different places it is used in across the organization, and where each use of the information is sourced from.

In my personal experience, the worst-case scenario was a company where one critical piece of data was recreated thirty-two times! A definite waste of time and resources. It also opened up a potential liability risk. While the information was derived correctly in most cases, there were a handful of instances where a mistake had been made and included in documentation that was issued outside the company. I have heard from other consultants instances of finding content duplicated as many as 40 or 50 times.

These instances can be resolved by using collaborative platforms where information can be searched for, accessed, and used across functional boundaries. Such information needs to be designed and written with potential reuse in mind (a topic covered in more detail in Chapter 10).

Knowledge sharing

The true business benefits of collaborative knowledge sharing, such as improved productivity, reduced cross-functional boundaries, and better access to customer feedback, often become lost to a perceived, and in many ways understandable, fear.

If you have knowledge, then share it. The community will benefit.

Basic reuse

To effectively take advantage of concepts like collaboration and knowledge sharing, the content you produce needs to be developed so that it can be reused in different documents or for different processes and applications.

In her blog,[1] fellow XML Press author Anne Gentle links to a story[2] about a family who, after ten years of maintaining a website on various ways to tie knots (which received four million visits a year), re-purposed that content into a popular iPhone app called Animated Knots.

Gentle summarizes their success factors as follows:

- **Persona-based:** First, they sound like they use persona-based design. They had four ideal audiences in mind: climbers, fishers, Scouts, and boaters. A surprising additional group they discovered later, and were proud to serve, were fire fighters and rescue workers.

- **Labor of love:** Also, they gave their content time – the original site was a labor of love for ten years. I'm sure they used both hard data like web analytics along with soft data like the incoming success stories from their main audience members to improve the content in that time.

- **Visual appeal:** They also use a lot of photos, which they shoot themselves.

- **Seasonal timing:** Their app was featured in the iTunes store during the U.S. summer months, which was just the right

---

[1] http://justwriteclick.com
[2] http://justwriteclick.com/2011/01/20/repurposing-and-reinventing-content/

content at just the right time for people enjoying the outdoors with their iPhones in tow.

- **An ecosystem with lots of adoption:** Martin Grogono, one of the family members explained that the iTunes store and high installed base of iPhone users was a boon to their app.

This is a great example of looking at ways to reuse and re-purpose your existing content, but not all reuse needs to be this dramatic. Even the simplest form of sharing content between documents can bring positive results. Perhaps the simplest and most common form of content reuse, which most people are familiar with, is the idea of copy and paste, where a selection of content from one document is copied and then pasted into a second document. In most cases this is done mainly as a productivity shortcut to avoid retyping information.

On a slightly more sophisticated level, you may have a source document, or even a simple database, that includes approved phrases, such as legal disclaimers, that need to be included in a series of documents or on a website.

The main problem with any sort of copy and paste operation is that neither the source, nor the target have any knowledge of each other. Once you have pasted the copied content into a new document, that new document has no link back to where that information came from, unless you manually add one.

So, let's say one of the disclaimers is updated by the legal department. How do you know, unless you kept a separate record, where that content was reused? Alternatively, let's say someone spots a typo in one of the disclaimers in a secondary document and corrects it. It probably isn't obvious that the original text was copied from elsewhere; so how do you get that correction back to the source and ensure it is propagated across all the places it is used?

Copy and paste reuse promotes static, or dumb, content, and the whole process becomes one of copy, paste, and forget. What is needed is a process that allows a copy, paste, and remember model. This is achieved by developing intelligent content.

Intelligent content

Leading content strategist, Ann Rockley describes intelligent content as:

 ...content which is not limited to one purpose, technology or output. It's content that is structurally rich and semantically aware, and is therefore discoverable, reusable, reconfigurable and adaptable. It's content that helps you and your customers get the job done. It's content that works for you and it's limited only by your imagination.[3]

In short, this means developing content that can be detached from its immediate context and used elsewhere. For instance, information such as a product name, which was originally created as text on a page of documentation, may also be usable in an information processing system, on a website, as part of marketing and product documents, or even as a data field in a online order processing and billing system.

---

[3] http://thecontentwrangler.com/2011/01/17/what-is-intelligent-content/

Reuse is best supported by using a markup language that allows you to tag content based on its type (part number, product name, etc.) rather than its format (italics, bold, etc.).

For example, a tag such as `<pn>` might be used to indicate a product name:

```
<pn>Acme Gadget Deluxe</pn>
```

Different systems can then be configured to use that content in different ways:

- For a print output document, the publishing tool could be instructed to print anything in a `<pn>` tag in italics.

- For a web site, a web delivery program could be instructed to use HTML/CSS code to display anything in a `<pn>` tag as bold and red.

- For a touch screen tablet computer app, the tag could indicate a link to launch a video about the product.

- For a billing application, that tag may link to a table entry in a database that includes pricing, in-stock status, etc.

Think of your content as Lego bricks. Lego uses one core concept, the simple interlocking brick, to create an almost infinite number of variations.

One potential problem with this approach is that you can end up with a vast number of "Lego bricks." To make the best use of this approach, your content needs to managed. There are many commercial content management tools available that can manage different types of content; most are tuned for particular types of delivery options, such as web site content management, technical documentation content management, etc. But for smaller amounts of data, content management could be something as simple as an Excel spreadsheet or a simple database.

Another consideration when developing intelligent content is authoring style. When creating this style of content you have to be aware that the information and content may be used elsewhere in a different context. In this instance, you need to avoid context-specific phrases and navigation pointers such as "see next page" or "as above," etc. The same applies to graphics, illustrations, or any content that may be used elsewhere.

Collaborative platforms

When it comes to setting up environments that promote the idea of shareable intelligent content, the first reaction tends to be to install technology in the form of one, or more, of the many different collaborative platforms available in today's market place. However, as The Content Wrangler, Scott Abel cautions in his intro to *WIKI: Grow Your Own For Fun and Profit*[15], beware of becoming addicted to software.

Throwing technology at a problem before you understand the business need, the processes, and the human factors can create more issues than it solves. I've sat in way too many meetings where more time was spent trying to figure out how to use a tool than on discovering ways a tool could bring benefits.

Before you consider software tools and collaborative platforms, you need to understand how people can contribute to, and share information, across your content development process. In addition to listening to how your customers consume your content, you should be listening and talking internally about how you create your content.

7

Consistency Saves You Money

How many times have you been in a meeting with a colleague discussing something at length only to find out that you've both been talking about the same thing, but using different words? Or conversely, thinking you are discussing the same thing, but finding out that different parts of the organization use the same word or phrase to actually mean two different things?

If you've ever heard the phrase "what we are arguing about here is semantics," then you have a communication problem. If it causes problems and confusion for you internally, what does it mean for your business partners and customers? Are semantics costing you money?

How do your customers experience your content? Have you ever gone to a website to order a product only to discover that the name used on the parts order form is different from that used on the marketing/sales pages of the site? Or called in to a support line only to find out that the name they use is different than the one in the manual that shipped with the product? Ever been on a training course where the trainer says something like "ignore what's in the documents"?

Even when a community or industry develops its own words and phrases through common usage (what may be perhaps best termed as jargon), you can't assume that everyone you deal with in that community uses that jargon in the same way or applies the same meaning. Sub-communities have a habit of taking such terms and adding their own spin and definitions that reflect their own common usage.

At the start of most projects one of the most useful questions to ask is "what do you mean by...?" Establishing a baseline of definitions can save a lot of wasted time and misunderstanding. But perhaps even more important is that once you have established a common vocabulary, you must use it consistently through content design, development, and delivery.

Simply put, consistency saves you money.

But, consistency is just one part of managing your content so that it can be reused, translated, leveraged, and consumed in the most effective manner.

The recipe for successful organization, management, and consistent use of your content includes:

- Clarity,
- Consistency
- Honesty,
- Findability

Clarity

In Chapter 4, I discussed in detail how you need to think about the language you are using in communicating with your customers and partners, especially across national and cultural boundaries. The same considerations apply within your organization too. Clarity of language and purpose is just as important when communicating and sharing content with colleagues. If you consider that everyone you communicate with is a customer, then you can go a long way to removing internal barriers.

Don't assume that the recipient of your document, email, etc., will be able to interpret what you mean; make the message simple and clear and avoid the risk of misinterpretation. If there's an easy way to say something using simpler words, then use it. More problems are caused by misinterpretation than by actual mistakes.

On a wider scale, clarity of language is vitally important for the effective reuse of content. You need to be able to find information to reuse, and know that when you do it will fit and work seamlessly in its new context.

Consistency

Call a spade a spade, not a personal manual earth moving device.

A company I worked with in the past employed several people whose job was to "translate" the names of parts on manufacturing drawings into what they felt were more user-friendly names for customers. At first pass this may seem like a smart idea, but it raised several issues:

- It introduced disparities between training, technical documentation (who used the new names), and spares ordering (linked to manufacturing database).

- There was no clear business need; no one had actually checked to see if the customers had an issue with the engineering terminology.

- Potential liability. In some cases the terms used by engineering were done to protect company intellectual property, and in other cases they reflected equipment names from supplier and vendor companies that were trademarked.

- The process created another information silo.

A better route would have been to collaborate with engineering and develop an common terminology database.

Sometimes such problems are the result of using disparate inform-ation systems in different parts of the organization. One example was caused by an engineering system that only had "X" characters in the "name" field. As a result, the engineering names were truncated into something like a text message. The customer-facing names were changed to add clarity, but there was no direct link between the new names and the system-limited ones. The root cause was different from the previous example, but the end result was the same – disparity, potential liability, and information silos.

You don't necessarily need to build large terminology databases or use software to manage and check terminology usage – al-though software is commercially available. Even something as simple as agreeing to consistently use a name created early in the development process throughout any downstream content cre-ation can have a positive impact.

One company I worked with actually got its name from a typo during the early stages of the product development process. The same misspelling was used so often that it became the initial product name and was eventually adopted as the company name.

Consider the following: if your engineering team decided to use "personal manual earth moving device" to describe a piece of equipment, and if they used that phrase consistently across all subsequent content, then if at a later date you decide to use "spade" instead, you could do a search and replace and be confid-ent that you had found all instances.

However, what if your training team unilaterally decided they didn't like "personal manual earth moving device" and used "shovel" in the training content, and then someone in technical documentation used "digging tool," and marketing used "Earth-Mover." Doing a search and replace for a new approved term would be almost impossible, unless you knew every possible variation used across the organization.

When everyone in your organization uses the same word or phrase, and you all know what it means, it is easier to organize, manage, and reuse your content.

Honesty

Above all, your content should be honest and, as far as possible, accurate. This may seem to be obvious in things like technical documentation, where dishonesty and inaccuracy can lead to possible injury, equipment damage, and potentially to liability issues, and lawsuits.

But I strongly believe that this tenet also applies to other more creative forms of corporate content development, such as marketing.

> I'm a writer; I take the truth and give it scope.
> —Paul Bettany as Geoffrey Chaucer in *A Knight's Tale* (2001)

If I have one underlying tenet that I try to live by, it's to tell the truth. It's a philosophy I also apply to my writing. Most of my published work[1] to date has been non-fiction, which by its very nature involves a lot of research and fact checking to make sure that what you are presenting is the "truth."

The problem with doing research based on historical events, and particularly in the case of biography, is that the "truth" is often

---

[1] http://alanjporter.com/

what the person telling the story believes to be true. For that reason, as much as possible, I try and go back to original sources and documents. The same thing applies when I'm writing fiction. I always try to stay truthful to the established rules of the fictional world I am working in. With a licensed property that also means researching the facts that other writers have established.

So, what has this got to do with corporate communications?

Over my years in corporate communications, as both employee and consultant, I have created a lot of marketing content: blog posts, Tweets, white papers, product literature, websites, and press releases. And, as with my other writing, I always try to tell the truth. Sure, as in the quote above, I sometimes take the truth and give it "scope." Yes, I'm perfectly happy saying that 10% is "double-digit growth" or that 51% equates to "most" or "the majority" because beneath the spin they are still verifiable facts.

Where I have problems is with marketing spin that uses absolute terms like unique, best-ever, ultimate, or first. if you want to use those terms, that's fine – but do some research and some fact checking to make sure that you really are the "first to market," or that what your product does really is "unique," and if what you are offering really is the "ultimate," are you really saying that you never intend to improve it?

This is even more important when you are marketing to an established audience that is familiar with the market segment, your products, and your competitors' products. Say the wrong thing or use the wrong word, and they will go check. If what you claim isn't true, they will call you out on it. That will undermine every other marketing message you put out.

One perceived falsehood can undermine the credibility of everything else you do. Misinformation and wrong perceptions have a habit of staying around and are very quick to be taken as fact. They have an alarmingly long shelf life and are difficult to correct.

There is no excuse for any marketing material not to tell the truth. Sure your readers may have to read between the lines or decipher the spin, but the foundation of what you are saying should always be verifiable.

Findability

No matter how good, informative, or useful your content is, it is useless if no one can find it, and that applies both inside and outside the organization. I discussed earlier that findability is an important consideration for those who consume your content outside your organization, but it is also key to any sort of successful collaboration within an organization.

Once you know what content you produce and what content you have, you need to name it and organize it so others can find it and reuse it.

This can be achieved by using some of the guidelines for language conventions already discussed, clarity and consistency, or through the use of tools.

You need to do an audit of where your content is stored and make sure that people who can reuse that information have access. Often access to content is restricted to particular project teams or functional groups, when others who might find the same content valuable cannot access it, or may not even be aware of its existence.

This is another instance where silos of information, even within the same project or functional department, can easily be created. People keep information on their own desktop or laptop machines, or they get passed around as email attachments to only a select few. Different pieces of content are stored on different systems.

But if you consider other internal functions and groups as if they were external customers looking for information, you can then look at how you organize your information with a more holistic view. In this instance you can use collaborative platforms for sharing content, such as a wiki or something like Google Docs; maybe incorporate search tools, keywords, and techniques such as tagging so that content is easier to find.

The easier information is to find, the easier it is to share and collaborate. The aim should be to move from recreating content many times over to creating something once, making it easy to understand and find, and promoting its reuse wherever it is appropriate.

I was once in a meeting and heard the following "That's a good internal tagline, but it doesn't mean anything to customers." It seemed obvious to me that the response in this situation should be to use the same terminology inside and outside the organization.

In short you need call a spade a spade. Make sure that everyone knows that it is called a spade, and also make it easy for them to find out where information about the spade is created and kept across the organization. With a consistent approach to the use of language and terminology you can see almost immediate benefits in content reuse, reduced support costs, and more accurate searches across both internal and external systems. Making it easier for your customers to find the right information, and for your staff to talk about your products or services in the same way that customers do can only lead to more revenue opportunities.

8

Where Are Your
Pain Points?

Over the preceding chapters I've presented and discussed several areas where you can focus on discovering what content you produce, how it's written, and how to organize and manage it. There's a lot to consider, and there are probably ways you can make improvements across your whole content design, development, and delivery process.

But you can't do everything at once. So how do you decide where, and how, to allocate resources to get the biggest, and possibly quickest, return on any investment in content improvement?

You need to identify your biggest, most serious content issues – your "pain points."

A "pain point" is anything that has a direct negative impact on any part of the content design, development, and distribution process or, most importantly, your revenue.

Potential pain points

The following are just some of the potential pain points that might affect your organization.

Content design

- Are you designing and delivering the right content, and is your content being used in the right places?

- Are you using the most useful, as opposed to traditional, content? Question the all too frequent statement, "we've always done it this way." What worked 5 or 10 years ago may no longer be effective.

- Have you considered accessibility needs? Can people who are deaf, blind, color blind, etc., access your information?

- Do you meet all applicable laws, industry regulations, and standards?

- Are you meeting all your contractual obligations? Do you know what those obligations are?

- Is your content stopping you from entering new markets due to industry jargon, translation issues, cultural barriers, etc.?

- Do you want to provide only the information specific to the version of the product that the customer owns? Without the information about options that they don't own? Or do you want to give just hints about what they don't have so you can up-sell?

- How do you handle content and information from third-party companies, vendors, suppliers, partners, and acquisitions, and just as important, how do you pass content on to your partners?

- Does your information model support all the products that may still be in use?

- Does your content model match your support model, and does your content strategy mirror it? Software companies I have worked with have had support policies with a two-year rolling window, while large equipment manufacturers tend to have a "as long as there is one operating anywhere in the world, we will support it" model, which can mean that support information needs to be maintained for decades.

- How about legacy data? Do you have old systems and content models that may include duplication of terms, serial numbers, names, etc., that you also use in more modern products?

- Are you creating content that says what your product does, rather than answering the question of how do I use it?

Content development

- Do you have content creation bottlenecks? Are there points in the process where everything gets funneled through one person or one small team? Do you have cross-functional dependencies that put a disproportionate work load on one particular group?

- Do your content developers have access to the products they are creating content about?

- Do you have the right people with the right skills? If you are planning to increase the number of graphics you use, do you have graphic designers on staff as well as traditional technical illustrators? Thinking of moving to video, animation?

- Do you have cross-fertilization of skills between the developers of technical and marketing content?

- Do your employees have the right information readily available? How much time is spent searching for information rather than using it to do their job ?

- Is your content driven by engineering and design? – Will that work for your customer? For instance, car manuals are written to a 5th grade reading level. Don't make assumptions about your audience based on your internal community.

- What's the reading level of the information in your content versus the average for your customers? A website I analyzed recently provided a service that was aimed at non-native English speakers, yet used language aimed at college-level, native English speakers.

Content distribution

- Is your content effective or does it fall short of its purpose? This can be identified from support calls, feedback from field sales and service team members, and from listening to customers themselves.

- Is your content being delivered to the right people through the right channels? Don't design and develop just for the web if the majority of your customers still use, and want, paper.

- How do you actually get the content into your customer's hands? Your responsibility doesn't stop with publishing content.

- Is the content in the right format or media to best deliver your message?

- Are you supplying your distributors and customers with the most accurate and up-to-date content?

One customer I worked with knew that everything they shipped to a customer was at least 30 days out of date when it shipped. Another major corporation would take between 90 and 120 days get a change to their website, while a direct competitor updated their 10,000 page website every 24 hours!

This is far from a fully comprehensive list, but it should get you thinking about the many factors that influence the design, creation, distribution, and consumption of your content.

How to identify pain points

One way to identify pain points is to take a close look at your current processes, starting with design and continuing through to distribution to customers, making sure you also look at how your customers access and use your content. Look at every aspect and document your "as is" process. The result needn't be large complex documents; in fact, flow charts often work best for this exercise. As you go through the process keep asking:

- Why do you do this step?
- Where does the information come from?
- What is this content designed for?
- Who will use this information (internally and externally)?
- Where will it be used? On a computer, a website, a tablet computer, or a sheet of rolled up paper in the back pocket of a mechanic's overalls?
- When will it be used?
- Is there a feedback mechanism?
- What does it contribute to the business process?

Once you understand your current process, you will start to see potential pain points. Conduct further analysis by looking at:

- Customer support calls,
- Negative field service and sales feedback,
- Internal bottlenecks,
- Incidences of apparent confusion.

For areas where you don't have direct visibility, you can use techniques such as:

- Web traffic analysis,
- Search term analysis,

- Competitive analysis,
- Surveys,
- Monitoring social networks, online groups, and communities,
- Active listening and talking to customers.

With your pain points identified, you can focus your efforts on those areas and manage them to get the best return on any improvements and changes you make.

Managing Your Content

9

Styles and Standards

The great thing about standards is that you have so many to choose from.

—Andrew Tanenbaum

I'm writing this chapter the week that NASA's thirty year Space Shuttle program comes to a close with the safe return of Atlantis and the crew of STS-135. The flight of the last Space Shuttle reminded me of a question I often ask when discussing the use of standards at conferences.

 What's the connection between a horse's backside and the Space Shuttle?

The answer goes something like this: horse to chariot; chariot to farm cart; farm cart to British trains; British trains to US trains, train gauge to tunnel width; tunnel width to booster rockets; booster rockets to Space Shuttle!

I'm not the first to ask the question, and I have heard many others use this illustration of how one technology can influence another, but it's an effective way of discussing the ongoing impact of standards. Although, to be honest, most of the underlying assumptions on these particular standards are in fact apocryphal and don't stand up to close scrutiny.[1] However, the central message of this is that once you develop a standard way of doing things, it can be shared with, and understood by, others.

---

[1] Historian Lindsay Powell examines this story in detail in his book *All Things Under the Sun: How Modern Ideas are Really Ancient*[17].

According to *Webster's Dictionary*[25][2] the word "standard" has several distinct meanings, but the two definitions that are relevant to this discussion are:

stan·dard (noun)

1. *That which is established as a rule or model by authority, custom, or general consent.*
2. *That which is established by authority as a rule for the measure of quantity, extent, value, or quality.*

Why we need standards

Standards are all around us, most of the time we don't notice their application; in fact it tends to be the reverse – we notice when something isn't done the way we expect it to be. As the first dictionary definition implies, not all standards are formal, in fact most of the ones that we interact with on a daily basis are developed through mutual consent or cultural customs.

But in business – especially when exchanging content, information, and physical products – the formal authoritative standards take on a greater role.

Consider for instance the humble nut and bolt. The makers of nuts and bolts want their products to have the widest use possible, while everyone, from building contractors to equipment manufacturers to weekend hobbyists, wants to know that if they buy and use certain size nuts and bolts they will fit, and that wrenches and other tools will be the right size to work with those parts.

---

[2] Webster's Revised Unabridged Dictionary, 1913 Edition. Even though this edition is nearly 100 years old, the meaning of the word "standard" is essentially identical to current definitions.

But even in something as simple as a nut and bolt, there are competing standards. Most today are designed to either a metric (based on millimeter measurements) or an imperial (based on fractions of a inch) standard. Yet even this simple divide can cause problems.

In my early aerospace days we had an incident when it was reported that the co-pilot's window on one of the aircraft types we supported had blown out on take-off. After a lengthy investigation it was determined the cause was the screws used to fix the windshield surround.

At the time of the incident the airline was in the process of replacing their aging fleet with newer aircraft. The older aircraft used imperial parts, while the newer ones had metric parts. Reportedly, some imperial screws had gotten accidentally mixed into the spares bin for the metric fleet and had been used to secure this particular windshield after a repair. It turns out the angle of the thread is slightly different between a metric and an imperial screw, just enough to form a minute air-pocket, so that when the aircraft took off the resultant change in air-pressure was enough to push the screws out.

The moral of this story is to, if possible, stick to one standard for one purpose, and if you are forced to use more than one standard at the same time, make sure you keep them as distinct as possible and have a clear migration path to move from the old standard to the new one. After all, standards are put in place to help prevent errors and mistakes.

Standards make things easier to create and easier to use because of familiarity and expectations. Consider the simple book. When the printing press was first developed and came into common use, there was no defined model for what a book should look like. But, over a period of several decades a model developed that became accepted practice and is still familiar to us centuries later. When we pick up a book we expect:

- A cover with the book's title and the name of the author.

- The title and author's name to be repeated on the spine so we can find the book when shelved.

- A title page inside with publisher's information.

- A table of contents.

- Contents divided into smaller chunks called Chapters.

- An index, if it's a non-fiction book.

- A back cover with some information about the book's contents.

Interestingly, we are going through a similar period of development with the rapid growth of eBooks. For the most part, what we are currently doing is applying the print book model to new delivery devices. If you read about the early history of print publishing[3] many of the concerns and arguments expressed are the same ones we hear today about eBooks. In some ways, nothing has really changed. In fact, devices like the Kindle are in reality little more than electronic page turners, rather than true eBooks. It may be that the page-based model will be the future, but personally I doubt it. I expect that with wider use, we will see the development of a new standard way of delivering content that makes the best use of the digital platform.

---

[3] I highly recommend Andrew Pettegree's *The Book in the Renaissance*[12], which covers the first 150 years of the arrival of printing technology in Western Europe and its political and social impact.

Standards also mean that things work as expected. Returning to the nut and bolt example, standards are the reason that the axiom of "tighty righty; loosey lefty" works. Imagine the chaos and frustration if the direction in which you turned a bolt to undo it depended on who the manufacturer was.

Standards are the basis of nearly all collaboration. You can't share information with someone else if they can't understand the way that information is presented to them. From the simple layout of a letter to the most complex digital exchange transactions, such as those taking place between various financial institutions, the sender and the recipient need to use the same rules.

Content standards

The effective use of standards for design, development, collaboration, and use apply equally to content as they do to nuts and bolts or a stock exchange trade.

There are a large number of different standards that can be applied to content, but most are devised and implemented for the following reasons:

- Improve quality
- Improve productivity
- Enable data exchange
- Improve enabling technology
- Enable accurate translation
- Provide consistent delivery

At conferences I often ask my audience what they think is the most widely adopted content standard. Often the answer is whatever technical standard is currently getting the most industry buzz, or sometimes someone will say it's HTML, the mark-up language that defines what a web page looks like. It's rare that someone will give what I believe to be the correct answer. It's the standard I used as an example earlier in this chapter, and the one that you are more than likely experiencing as you read this – the printed book.

My point in asking this question is to emphasize that no matter how much we think, and talk, about standards as technology-driven, they are more usability-driven, and the ones that are the most successful are those that, like the book, evolve over time rather than derive from some sudden technological revolution. Ideally, standards should be driven by usability and allowed to mature over time.

For instance, my wife works within the legal administration system of the local county. The county's legal code, written in the 1980s, specifically states that electronic copies of court proceedings should be kept on 5.25 inch diskettes. (Remember those?) Now in practice, they haven't done that in years, so technically the current incarnation of the county court is breaking its own law. (At least for the moment, my wife is part of a team currently revising the county code to remove such time-sensitive technological restrictions.) Conversely, there are some examples where they could be using technology to do things more efficiently, but the rules, or standards, mandate a process with specific manual steps.

As the quote at the top of this chapter states, the great thing about content standards is that there are so many to choose from. There are standards covering every part of the design, develop, delivery cycle. Standards covering text, graphics, data exchange, content management, translation, formatting, delivery to different devices, usability, accessibility, and so on.

The thing to remember is that you will need to choose different standards to meet the business needs of different parts of the content life cycle. As Sandy Ressler points out in *Perspectives on Electronic Publishing*[18], "A single standard cannot possibly satisfy all requirements all the time. To believe any one standard is a magic bullet is foolish."

Most standards have some value under certain circumstances. Very few are valuable under many circumstances. So how do you pick the right ones?

A strategy for picking standards

Before discussing the things you need to think about when choosing a set of standards, there are three mind sets that can distort your perspective on standards:

- The technology bigot
- Member of the Standard of the Month Club
- The person who doesn't realize that standards exist

I will freely admit to have been a member of all three at various points in my career.

"Technology bigots" are so enamored of a particular technology solution that they insist you should use only that technology, and design your process to meet the particular needs of that technology. People with this viewpoint often lose sight of the business need and become distracted and focused on the minutiae of the technology in question. When discussing standards they will only consider ones that their favorite technology supports, rather than looking for a standard, and supporting technology, that meets the business needs.

Members of the "Standard of the Month Club" like to be up on the latest industry trends and buzz. They often think that the solution currently getting the most coverage at conferences and trade shows is a "one-size-fits-all" solution. As discussed above, there is never a single solution that does this. The hottest standard may have some good ideas you want to consider, but it doesn't automatically mean it's the right fit for your situation.

At this point, I doubt you are one of the "people who don't realize that standards exist," but you are likely to run into one or more over the course of any standards-related project.

So having put those three considerations in place, what should you be looking for?

As with many other activities in developing a strong content strategy, you need to ask yourself a lot of questions:

- Is there a long term support requirement?

- Is there a need to produce multiple deliverables from the same content?

- What's the content production cycle?

- Do you need to incorporate content from other sources?

- How will the content be delivered?

- Who revises and uses the content?

- Does the content need to be translated?

- Do you have budget to do implement new standards?

- Can you justify any return on investment (i.e. reduced support calls, lower translation costs, etc.) from implementing a standards based approach?

- Do you need new software or hardware?

- What's the timescale for implementing a standard? Can you take a phased approach?

- Are any standards contractually or industry mandated?

- Do people have sufficient expertise to implement the selected standards?

- Do you need to develop specialists in your organization to assist in the implementation and enforcement of selected standards?

- How will the adoption of the standard affect the format of current deliverables?

- How will you enforce the standards, especially when they affect so many different people in so many different parts of the organization?

- What parts of the organization and process will this impact?

For this last question, you need to do some lateral thinking and go back to a holistic view of your content and how it is designed, developed, and used throughout your organization. Here's one example from my own experience. When a technical publications department I was working with introduced the use of Simplified Technical English (see Chapter 4), it caused confusion in the engineering department, which was tasked with reviewing and approving the documentation for technical accuracy. The engineers took it on themselves to rewrite the documentation back into "engineering speak" causing major delays in approvals and much heated discussion between the engineers and technical writers. Once the engineers had spent a half-day on an overview training session, they then understood the need for, and use of, a controlled language. Being aware of this peripheral impact early on, and keeping the affected engineers informed of the standards selection process, would have helped eliminate the delays that resulted from just throwing the process change at them with no preparation.

A process for picking a set of standards

Once you have answered and thought through the questions above, you will have a clearer idea of the business needs the standards you want to use have to meet. You will also have a clear view of the sorts of technology tools you will need. With these in mind you can move onto the next steps, but remember at all times to keep the end goal in mind, as this is what drives the best standards selection, not the technology.

- **Look at a selection of standards:** For instance, if you have decided you need some sort of terminology control and a simplified language set to aid translation costs, take a look at the various standards out there. Maybe Simplified Technical English (STE) is for you, maybe not – maybe just adopting the Government's Plain Language initiative will be enough.

- **Research the possibilities:** Once you have shortlisted some standards, do your research on each.

- **Talk to people who have implemented those standards:** Look at how other people have implemented the standard. Why did they pick this one? What business issue were they trying to solve? Did it work? Did they get the expected results? What was involved in implementing it? What was easy? What was hard? People love to share their stories, and most will be happy to share their experiences.

- **Understand the assumptions underlying the standard:** Understand what the standard is designed to do. Don't get distracted by the "cool stuff" it will allow you to do, unless that "cool stuff" solves an immediate, or well-defined future, business need.

- **Have an open mind about standards:** Keep your goal in mind. Think, "we need a standard to do X," not, "we need to implement standard Y."

- **Make sure the standard is complete for your needs:** If you think something's missing from a standard,then don't use it.

- **Make sure you have an exit strategy for your content:** Make sure that any standard you are considering gives you a way to move your content. Remember, you don't want your data to be locked on laser-disc or 5.25 inch floppy discs. Nor do you want your content locked into a proprietary software format. Consider your growth plan. At some point you may decide to move into a new industry that has different standards, and you don't want your content to be a road block just because it's in another format or standard,

- **Consider whether you need a multi-step adoption process:** Your starting point (your "as-is" process) may dictate which standard you can pick. If the leap is just too big to go from your "as-is" to your desired "to-be," then you may want to plan an evolution process that takes place in several steps, migrating from one standard to another as you go.

- **Make sure the standard is viable:** That is, make sure it is actively maintained and supported within its community.

- **Remember:** The most successful and enduring standards are evolutionary rather than revolutionary.

Company style guides

So far I've been discussing external standards. That is, ones that exist in your industry or have been developed, through custom or design, by communities with a shared interest in solving a particular issue or meeting a particular need. But, the most effective standard is often an internal company style guide (or perhaps a series of style guides.)

You probably already have some of these in place. Some may be formal documents, while others are community-driven based on people's experience and expectations.

Be aware that if many of your practices are based on a notion of "we have always done it that way," you should re-examine those underlying assumptions. As illustrated at various points earlier in this book, expectations, usage, audiences, and technology change; and what may have made sense years before may no longer apply.

On a recent consulting engagement, while looking at the company's style guide, I noticed an entry that stated that a certain type of image had to be a particular size. It turned out that this size would work well on a printed page but would be unreadable on a mobile device. No matter how many times I asked why it had to be this specific size, no one could give me an answer beyond "that's just the way it has to be."

Eventually the customer's team came to the realization that no one in the company actually knew the reason for that specific limitation. And when we changed it, nothing in the process broke. In fact it made some parts of it more efficient because they no longer had to store and manage different versions of an image locked at different sizes. Now they could use one image and resize it on the fly when it was about to be displayed, printed, etc.

The best internal style guides are those that are good enough to help with consistency and messaging, but not so strict that they make the job harder and distort the message.

So, if you don't already have some internal style guides in place, how do you go about building them? The following are a few suggestions for possible approaches:

- **Use industry standards as a baseline:** You may find an industry standard that's close to what you need, but not a perfect fit. In that case you could deviate from it and use the industry standard as your baseline. But if you do, make sure you understand the impacts of that deviation, especially if at some point you intend to exchange content with someone else who uses that same standard.

- **Build template libraries:** Let your content creators focus on content, not format, and use templates to define look and feel.

- **Use collaborative working spaces:** Development of standards through consensus is a common way to build a style guide. I've seen this done using collaborative platforms like wikis or by holding summits where a group gets together in a conference room for a couple of days and simply hashes out a first pass at a style guide.

- **Treat your business like a franchise:** Think about how you would communicate what you do so that someone else could repeat it. That's the way that franchise operations work. Everything is described and repeatable. In fact, fast food restaurants are some of the best examples of effective standards and style guides at work. So even though it may be for internal use only, write a franchise document. But, write it like it's public, and then see if new employees can understand and work to the same standards.

However you decide to create your own style guides and internal standards, once you have them in place, don't dictate their use: explain and demonstrate the benefits. Not just the immediate benefits to the content designers and creators, but the downstream benefits as well. Show how standards are part of an overall, holistic content strategy.

Don't forget ripple effects

Standards and style guides apply to the use of graphics as much as text, multimedia, or any other part of your content pool. In fact you are more likely to already have a graphics style guide than another type of style guide. The marketing department will most likely have a set of rules on how and where the corporate logo can be used. Think about extending that thinking to the business as a whole. Not just the logo, but fonts, symbols, icons, numbering schemes, and even colors.

However, be aware that the use of graphics may be a lot more pervasive across your company than you think. Consider the cost of even a small change to a graphics standard and its ripple effect. One major corporation decided to change its logo from a perfectly vertical stanch to having a 10-degree lean to the right because some advertising consultant had persuaded the CEO that this would signify that the company was "on the move" and "forward looking." No other change – just that 10 degree lean. It ended up costing the company over $20 million. Just think about all the places where your company logo is used. It's not just on your website or your business cards. In this case, there was also brick & mortar store signage, vehicles, uniforms, product packaging, even the signage at a sports arena they sponsored. And so it went on.

These sort of ripple effects can easily be triggered and run up large unseen costs. When developing standards, and particularly introducing new ones, don't forget to figure these effects into your thinking.

While ripple effects can be broad and expensive, you can minimize them in the future by adopting a create once, use many philosophy for your content.

Conclusions

All the above may seem like a lot to work through to ensure that you select the right standards to meet your business need, but the more due diligence you apply to the selection of content standards, then the greater the business benefit.

Behind all of the above are five key points that everything else is related to. If you only remember these five things, then you will be on the right road to improving the way you design, develop, and deliver your content:

- Remember that different standards are often meant to operate in different areas.

- Understand why a standard was created.

- Know what business need you are trying to solve, not what technology you want.

- Don't listen to "buzz" – research and make up your own mind.

- Try to manage change to minimize impact.

And above all remember the space shuttle and the horse: standards can have a long-term impact.

10

Rewrite and Reuse

Just few months after I graduated college and was starting out my aerospace career, I was asked to help out in one of the most tedious exercises I have ever been involved with. One of the older types of aircraft we no longer built, but still supported, needed a minor change. Due to an electrical short, a circuit breaker panel in the cockpit had to be moved from an overhead panel to a side panel. A distance of about six inches. The circuit breaker had been in its original position for over twenty five years, but we now had to issue revisions to every piece of aircraft documentation that mentioned that particular circuit breaker.

It took three of us four days to literally thumb through twenty five years worth of published hard copy paper aircraft manuals in the archives just to build a list of what would be affected. Once the change had been made, it took another two weeks before new pages were completed and ready to be sent out to the few remaining airlines still using that model of aircraft.

A few years later, when things were a bit more automated, we had a similar need to relabel a cockpit circuit breaker on one of the new aircraft we were building. It took a technical illustrator about five minutes to change the labeling on the appropriate graphic; it then took him about thirty seconds to log that updated graphic into the content management database. When the next revision cycle was run for any given airline, that update was automatically included in any relevant documentation.

A move to a reusable content model had saved us hundreds of hours and ensured that any published content was up to date with the latest available information.

In the first case every instance was a standalone individual re-creation of the same piece of information, with no relationship to any other copies. In the second case, there was a single instance of the content that could be reused across multiple deliverables with that relationship captured and stored.

The four key parts to making this sort of approach possible:

- Independent content
- Structured content development
- Content management
- Managing the change in approach

Independent content

Before you can give any serious thought to reusing your content across the organization and in different deliverables, you first need to separate your content structure from the format in which you create it.

When we write something with a standard word processor, we use formatting as a way to show the reader the structure of the content. For instance in this book, we use bold characters of a different size to indicate different types of headings. This is a common practice, and in most cases, this is how that rendering is achieved:

You type a piece of text, such as "New Section," that you want to be a heading in your document.

Then you highlight it with your cursor, maybe increase the font size a little, and then select Bold to make it look like this:

New Section

Good enough? Well yes, but only as long as that information is only to be parsed by human eyes. When we look at a document, or any content, we use visual clues such as bolding, font size, and indentations to determine its structure. It's a way of helping us decide what is more important and what pieces of content relate to each other.

Consider the typical business letter, which will most likely have structure shown in Figure 10.1:

```
LETTER
      HEADING
             DATE
             ADDRESS
                    TO
                    COMPANY
                    STREET
                    CITY
                    ZIP
      BODY
             SALUTATION
             SUBJECT
             PARAGRAPHS
      SIGNATURE BLOCK
             NAME
             TITLE
             COMPANY NAME
```

Figure 10.1. Business letter structure

Now, say we wanted to reuse some of the content of that letter in a different context, maybe as part of a website. We could just copy and paste, then reformat it to meet the presentation needs of the website (maybe a different font size, etc.). That is, perhaps, okay in a one-off instance, but if you want to do that sort of sharing on a larger scale, it would be better if the separate pieces of the content could be marked in a way that told us something about the information contained within as well as its place in a structure.

For instance let's say the letter included a section like the one shown in Figure 10.2:

> **New Part Numbers:**
> Due to a design change, all new products manufactured after January 1st, 2011 will use the New Widget (PN: 6789) instead of the Old Widget (PN: 1234).

Figure 10.2. Reusable content

This is information that might be useful to use elsewhere, and it would also be useful if we could search and find easily.

If we take the same information and add tags to it, we can then store it independently of the tool used to create it in the first place. Figure 10.3 shows how this might work.

```
<DesignChange>
  <Subject>New Part Numbers</Subject>
  <Para>Due to a design change, all new
    products manufactured after
    <date>January 1st, 2011</date>
    will use the <part>
       <partname>New Widget</partname>
       <partno>(PN: 6789)</partno></part>
    instead of the <part>
       <partname>Old Widget</partname>
       <partno>(PN: 1234)</partno></part>.
  </Para>
</DesignChange>
```

Figure 10.3. Markup for reusable content

If the information is stored this way in a content management system, then it would be easy to find it when doing a search for Design Changes, Dates, or Parts information.

If we want to display it in different locations, then each display environment can be programmed to read the tags – the information between the < > angle brackets – in a different way. For instance:

- The letter might render the Subject line as Arial 12 pt, bold, with the part numbers in italic.

- A website might display the Subject as Verdana 11pt, in bright red, and make the part numbers into hyperlinks to an online parts catalog.

- A manufacturing process document might just add the whole Design Change section as a NOTE section and make it all italic using a different color for the text.

All of this can be done without having to copy and reformat the information.

Tagging this way doesn't mean your content creators need to learn all the appropriate tags. This is done by experts, usually called Information Architects, who can examine sets of documents and build tag sets and structures that meet the needs of both reuse and publishing. Your content creation tools can then be set up to hide these tags from the user.

What will be required is that content creators use the tools in a consistent, structured manner using things such as styles and templates. For instance, instead of making a piece of text into a heading by just highlighting it and making it bold, they will need to select the correct type of heading (Heading1, Heading 2, etc.) from the style drop down. To input information about a manufacturing part, you may have added a "Parts" style that opens a dialog prompting them to supply a part name and number.

This sort of markup gives your content contextual freedom.

The most common tagging language used in business today is the eXtensible Markup Language, more commonly known as XML. XML allows you to detach information from its immediate context and use it elsewhere. as David Kelly says in, The Promise of XML Publishing,[1] "One of the great powers of XML is to free information from being merely text on a page, and give it other kinds of roles."

In fact, XML is now not only used as the basis of information interchange of text-based content, but also for applications as diverse as financial transactions and interprocess communication between software programs.

While a tagging scheme like XML works well for text, you also need to consider ways of reusing graphics across different sets of content. In Chapter 6, I discussed the use of symbols as a powerful way of reusing one image in multiple places to reinforce an idea or concept.

Building graphical libraries of symbols and generic views can also add to reuse. When developing generic views, you need to consider the level of detail to show. As a simple rule, the less detail, the more places the graphic will apply. But conversely, you have to make sure the graphic is recognizable and serves the intended purpose wherever it appears.

When you are reusing graphics, you also need to consider the translation impact and context of any associated text. A couple of ways to handle text in reusable graphics are:

---

[1] http://www.scriptorium.com/2010/09/the-promise-of-xml-publishing

- **Separate Layers:** Place the text on a separate layer (or overlay) in the graphics editing tool. This way if changes or translation of the text is needed, you only need to change one layer, not the complete graphic.

- **Callouts:** Instead of labels, add callouts such as (A), (B), etc., to the graphic, then in a table associated with, but separate from, the graphic, add the required item labels. This way any translation or changes affect the table, with no changes needed to the graphic.

Naming conventions

Sometimes basic reuse can be facilitated by something as simple as a file naming and numbering scheme for both text and graphics.

For instance the Air Transport Authority has a simple system that is used on all documentation related to civil aircraft. Originally designed for paper based manuals, each Chapter number was assigned a particular meaning. For instance, Chapter 28 was always about Fuel Systems, irrespective of which aircraft manufacturer the document came from, Chapter 57 was wings etc.[2]

The scheme was extended into a full six-figure breakdown that also designated systems and subsystems, so that a particular part or system could be described by an XX-XX-XX type numbering code that anyone familiar with that industry would understand. Many manufacturers and suppliers apply the same numbering scheme to file names for text and graphics, so that if you were

---

[2] A breakdown of the ATA Chapter Numbering scheme can be found at http://en.wikipedia.org/wiki/ATA_chapter_numbers

looking for a graphic about a Fuel System Pump, you would know to look for the code 284211 in the file name.

Structured content development

As discussed above, for your content to be truly independent of format, it needs some sort of underlying structure that can be marked up and managed. But before you rush headlong into tagging your content, you need to consider exactly what sort of structure you want to employ.

There are a lot of pre-developed structures, or "schemas" in XML terminology, available, and it may be that one or more of them will work for you. However, as with other areas of content design, you need to be cognizant of the underlying philosophies.

Some of the more popular approaches are topic-based, task-based, and minimalism. The three aren't mutually exclusive, and practices from one can be used in others. For instance, minimalism can be applied equally well to either topic-based or task-based content.

Topic-based structure

The basic idea here is to create a series of self-contained Topics, each covering one particular concept or idea, that then can be reused in different document sets or deliverables.

The most popular application of this type of structure is the Darwin Information Typing Architecture (DITA)[3] which specifies three different types of topics:

TASK   A topic that describes how to accomplish a task.

CONCEPT   A topic that contains definitions, rules, guidelines, and/or background information.

REFERENCE   A topic that describes reference information like command syntax, programming instructions, or detailed factual reference material.

DITA has seen a rapid growth in popularity and adoption, and many technical editing tools, publishing engines, and content management systems now support it.

Task-based structure

A task-based structure manages content at a finer level of granularity and is focused more on procedural information, where each block of content is a self-contained unit that describes how to complete a specific task. It may also include references to other tasks.

The idea is that when a technician needs to undertake a specific operation, say a repair, then all those references are resolved and added to the deliverable to provide a complete set of instructions on hand, without having to pull information from multiple different sources.

---

[3] http://dita.xml.org

Perhaps the best example of a task-based structure approach is the international specification known as S1000D.[4] Originally designed for aircraft maintenance, it has since become widely adopted in many industries where equipment maintenance and the management of spare parts is key.

Minimalism

Minimalism is also based on the idea that information should be delivered in short self-contained chunks, rather than lengthy narrative styles. Originally proposed as a way to design training materials, its principles have been adopted across other areas of content development. Minimalism is more of a concept than a strictly defined set of rules

Whatever approach to structured content you decide on, it must be considered up front as you define your content strategy and move towards content reuse. It doesn't work if applied as an afterthought. If you do try and apply a structure and tagging later, you may free your content from its formatting, and as a consequence gain some benefit, but you won't be able to leverage it as much as if you had fully planned things from the start.[5]

---

[4] The author was involved in the early development of the Aircraft Maintenance Task Orientated Support System (AMTOSS) which was the precursor of what developed into the S1000D standard.

[5] The traditional publishing industry (books, magazines etc.) is starting to see the benefits of an XML approach to tagging data when converting their content to eBooks. At the time of writing most publishing houses are adopting an XML-last approach to the publishing process where they are separating the content from the format after initial publication. A few are adopting a full XML-first process and using tagging from the outset. Publishers using an XML-first philosophy are seeing a much lower cost in preparing material for distribution to new digital platforms.

Reuse

When analyzing your content with a view to reuse, consider other places it might be used. Look at similar content and ask whether it really needs to be re-created or can it be replaced by information from elsewhere? You may also want to consider if you want your content structure to mirror the physical structure of your product. That sounds like it would be a given, doesn't it?

But have you ever tried to do any work on a modern car? Ever had to remove a wheel to change a water hose? Or how about taking off an air filter to change the spark plugs? When I was younger, I wouldn't think anything of pulling an engine out of a car and doing a complete rebuild; in fact that's how my friends and I spent many a weekend. These days the only time I pop the hood is to top off the windshield washer fluid. Cars are designed to go together in a way that provides the most efficient manufacturing process. Engine bays are crammed full of things to make the most use of the available space. They are not designed to allow you access. Maintenance and repair is a dealer-only activity, and the only thing a consumer is expected to do is top off fluids.

But if your content that describes that car is structured to reflect the manufacturing process, then how will the owner's manual look when he or she wants to find out how to top off the washer fluid or what switch does what? How will the information supplied to the dealer's technicians look in a world where disassembly is no longer simply the opposite of assembly.

Having a manufacturing or engineering driven content structure can also open up potential intellectual property issues. Consider using a 3D engineering drawing to provide the visuals in a new on-line service manual. Looks very cool, saves redrawing multiple illustrations, and is a great example of repurposing and reuse; but do you want a file out in the public domain that has all your manufacturing dimensions, tolerances, etc? There are solutions for this particular issue – one common one is the "simplified shareable model" approach – but it does illustrate a point about the ripple effects of using content in other areas. You need to weigh the many advantages of reuse against the occasional potential disadvantage.

In some cases, I have seen companies with multiple, distinctly different, content structures, one for engineering, one for service/support, and even one for marketing and sales. In such instances you need to have a process for systematically mapping content and its reuse from structure to structure.

It is also worth noting, as Sarah Maddox points out in her book, *Confluence, Tech Comm, Chocolate*[8]:

 There are arguments for and against content reuse. On the plus side, it can save time and promote efficiency. … On the other hand, the content may lose so much contextual information that it becomes difficult or impossible for the reader to understand. … Sometimes, the very mechanism of content reuse requires so much upkeep that it undoes any good it has done.

In my opinion, content reuse has its place. The most important thing is to get the design right. It must be clean and simple so that writers have minimal overhead in maintaining the reusable sections. … The solution is smart design of the reused chunks, achieved by consultation and iterative design.

Content management

It is no good separating your content structure from its format and tagging it without having a way to manage the resulting content chunks and where they are reused.

As with many other aspects of developing a strategy to leverage your content to its maximum potential, you need to consider content management from a business perspective. Things to consider include:

- Business requirements for content reuse.

- Translation needs.

- Multi-platform delivery options.

- Location of contributors.

- Integration into other systems and processes.

- Cost and expected Return On Investment (ROI)

- Any potential risk of having data in a central location. – Remember the need for a back-up / recovery process.

- Hosting scenarios – local hosted, hosted by a vendor in a remote data center, or even a cloud-based option.

Once you have decided you need a content management solution, you also need to consider the following:

- **Where used?** You need to track where content is reused, and conversely what content a particular deliverable reuses. This is essential for managing the impact of a change. Once you know where something is used across your content set, you can see the potential ripple effect and hopefully the potential savings too.

- **Database of agreed phrases / symbols:** If you are using a controlled language approach, or taking a more graphical approach to content sharing, you will need to develop and manage a database of agreed phrases, terminology, and symbols to be used across your content set. You may also have a database of legal content, safety notices, logos etc, that is prepared centrally and needs to be applied consistently across all your content.

- **Search:** Think about how your content designers, developers, and distributors will want to search for content that needs to be reused. Are they used to a more flexible Google type search, or are they used to more structured, formal naming conventions. Make sure that while you are managing your content it remains findable.

- **Visual indication of shared content:** Ideally your content developers and distributors should be able to easily determine if the content they are working on was sourced from elsewhere. They should also be able to easily determine what the ripple effect will be if they make a change to that content (assuming they have the permissions to do so). In some instances this can be done using icons in the content margins or by presenting shared content in a different color than the surrounding text.

- **Locking of content so only approved people can change the source:** Any reasonable content management strategy must consider access permissions. For both legal and safety reasons you probably don't want all your content developers to be able to change all the content they have access to.

- **Translation management:** Translation is not simply a matter of creating something in language A and having it converted to language B. In a structured reuse model, you also need to keep track of what pieces of content have been translated in relation to what usage. Coordinating content management correctly with translation management can mean drastic savings in translation costs, as you only translate smaller chunks of information as they are created or changed. You aren't paying to re-translate the same content over and over again.

- **CRUD:** Think about how you want to manage the whole content life-cycle process, from Creation to Reuse to Update to Disposal. Make sure you can identify changes and inform others so they can see what's new, changed, or deleted since they last accessed that information.

- **Mergers & Acquisitions / Business Partnerships:** How do you merge information coming in from other companies into your corporate data? How do you provide information that others use? Do you use exchange standards (a standard can be between just two organizations – as long as it is agreed to early). Is content exchange a contractual issue? Whatever process, there will be a cost impact, so you should consider how can you use content management techniques to minimize that impact.

Whatever approach you choose for content management, there will most likely be a tool available for it, but the most important thing to remember is that when you are considering a CMS, you should first focus on developing a thorough Content Management Strategy before choosing and implementing a Content Management System. The software vendors CMS (system) should support your CMS (strategy), not the other way around.

When it is time to choose a Content Management System you will find there are plenty available. I'll cover more on choosing the right technology solutions in Chapter 13.

Managing the change

During a client meeting a few months ago a senior manager on the project made this very astute observation:

> The technology is easy, the business process is the hard part.

He was, and is, correct. Once you have a strategy in place, one of the biggest challenges is helping people change the way they think and work. At the heart of managing that change is making people realize that what they are creating has potential beyond its immediate use, and that the content they are creating can be of benefit to someone, or somewhere, else in the organization.

Most people work within the constraints of their current assignment, project, or department. But by opening people up to a more holistic view they will start to see the benefits of collaboration, reuse, and adding intelligence to their content.

Separating the content from formatting can be a wrench for some who may see it as "de-skilling" their job. Many content creators take great pride in their skills at layout and design. In those cases it may be best to redirect those skills away from content creation to either content design or content delivery. Moving people out of their traditional roles into new roles where their skills can be used and where they can meet new challenges will go a long way to offsetting the feeling that new processes are being forced on them.

This raises a crucial point: new or substantially changed content strategies should be introduced using standard change management methodologies and not imposed "out of the blue." I have led too many software training courses where the answer to questions like, "why are you on this course" or "why are you adopting this tool," was "I don't know, the boss just told us we had to attend."

It isn't possible to involve everyone intimately with every stage of developing and implementing a switch to a reuse based content strategy. But everyone should be kept briefed, and people with particular skills or interests should be involved when, and where, they can add insight and value to the discussions.

And remember, it's not just about changing the way you work within your own organization, it's also about changing the way you exchange or accept content within your industry, with business partners, and even through a mergers and acquisitions process.

Laying the foundations to make your content intelligent will produce benefits for you across your organization and across all your business practices.

11

Answers are the Answer

When I first started out in content development I found that I really enjoyed writing what we called in the office "D&O" topics. Description and Operation documents were narrative text that described a particular system and the theory behind the way it worked. I really enjoyed doing the research and talking to the designers and engineers. I was also proud of the narrative text and graphics I produced, which showed just how clever those designers and engineers were.

Right up until I met the "purple monkey."

Over lunch one day, one of the senior technical writers at the company was telling me how much he enjoyed reading a particular D&O section I had written. But then he added, "but you know no-one reads those things." I must admit to being a bit taken aback by the revelation, and I asked him how he knew.

Back in the office he pulled one of the printed manuals, opened it to a D&O section he'd written a couple of years before, pointed to a paragraph at mid-page, and asked me to read it. There, buried in a sentence and completely out of context, was the phrase "purple monkey." He told me that in the two years that document had been in circulation, no-one had mentioned it or complained. He then told me he had used the same phrase in at least another six instances and had never heard any feedback or comment.

The thing is, he was right. No-one ever did read those lovingly crafted D&O sections. Once the information went electronic and we could track page visits, they got almost, and in some cases exactly, zero traffic.

Why was that?

Simply put, most content, especially that aimed at your customers, should be about "How" first and "What" second.

The word "How" always reminds me of a TV show I used to watch growing up in the UK. "HOW" ran for 15 years from the mid-sixties and on through the seventies. It has a simple premise, a panel of regular presenters would each ask a question starting with the word "How," the idea being that the answers would be entertaining and informative facts about science, history, mathematics, and simple puzzles. I remember rushing home from school twice a week to watch that show. I felt I was learning more from the answers to the word "how" than from being "told" facts and figures in my formal lessons.

And that is what most people want to know, answers to the question "how?"

When you open a box with a new product, what's the first question?

"How do I connect this all up?"

Then you want to know – "How do I switch this on?"

And "How do I make this work? How do I program it? How do I get it going?" and so on.

The problem is that until fairly recently most content supplied to users and consumers has been like my D&O topics: descriptions of what something does, loving text about how great the item is, and lists of features and functions, menu items, buttons, etc.

The thing is, by the time customers buy your product they know what it does. That's why they bought it in the first place; it solved a particular problem. So why tell them all that again? What they need to know is HOW to use it to solve that problem.

Don't show off what you know, show off how you can help. It's not about you showing what an expert you and your team are, it's about communicating with the customer.

Over the last couple of weeks I have purchased a new blu-ray player from Panasonic and a new Roku box for streaming internet video to my TV. The two sets of accompanying documentation provide a perfect illustration of "what" vs "how."

The Panasonic comes with a traditional paper Owner's Manual. All 36 paper pages of it.

The cover includes the model number and a nice welcoming message:

> Dear customer
>
> Thank you for buying this product.
>
> For optimum performance and safety, please read these instructions carefully.
>
> Before connecting, operating or adjusting this product, please read these instructions completely.

Turning the page you are confronted with all types of Safety Notices in a font so small it's almost impossible to read. Then a section on what Accessories I should have bought, followed by a couple of pages showing me what the buttons on the remote and device do (even though they are actually labeled on the player itself.) It's page 8 before we get the first "how do I?" answer with instructions on connecting the cables, and it's page 14 before we get to actually putting a DVD in the device.

In contrast the Roku "manual" was a glossy card folded three times to fit in the box. On the front it says:

> Get Started
>
> 1. Plug In
> 2. Connect
> 3. Watch

And that's what you get.

One "page" on what you should find in the box.

One "page" with a color-coded guide to the connection jacks.

And three "pages" that tell you how to plug the wires in, connect to your wireless network, and start watching.

Perhaps this change in approach is best summed up by a senior manager at an engineering company who told me that they had "Changed our focus and process from supporting the content creator to supporting the content user."

How to find the "How"

It's all too easy to do a features and functions list or a menu-by-menu breakdown. Finding out the questions that need answering is harder, but it's not impossible.

Start by listening to your customers. Look at typical support calls. See what questions people are asking in online forums, users groups, chat rooms, and on social media. You are monitoring all those for mentions of your company and products aren't you?

Look at the content that your users are creating themselves – a subject I will cover in more depth in Chapter 12. For instance, most of the informal user-generated instructional videos on YouTube are answers to "how to" questions.

You need to be your own "awesome dudes." The "awesome dude" tag is one I borrowed from my niece. Back in July, 2010 she posted the following on her Facebook status: "I finally have picture messaging on my Nokia N900 thanks to an awesome dude and his step-by-step YouTube video!!"

This simple message was one of the catalysts that started me thinking about this aspect of developing your content strategy.

Rather than use the manufacturer's instructions or look for an answer on their web-site or on-line help, my niece turned to the Internet and the wider online community. Her answer came not from Nokia, but from some "awesome dude" on YouTube.

The truth is you probably have the information to answer these sort of "how to" questions, but it may not be phrased right. A large percentage of support and customer care calls is spent just looking up information that is already there.

And as the "awesome dude" story shows, different answers to "How" may need different media approaches; text, graphics, animation, video, or audio. Your audience's culture and the context can make a difference.

Of course, one of the best ways to discover what questions you need to answer is to walk away from the computer and go talk to the people who use your content.

12

User-Generated Content

In the later years of high school, like many teenage boys, a lot of my life revolved around mending old cars. Most of my reading in those days was Haynes repair manuals[1]. Tucked away in the back of those manuals was a postcard on which you could send in your own tips, tricks, and corrections to the procedures. I don't know how many of those greasy thumb-print covered cards my friends and I sent in over the years, but I do recall our celebration the day we found one of our tips included in an updated version of one of the manuals.

To many this concept of "user-generated content" is often cited as potentially undesirable, as it is felt that such "unofficial" contributions will devalue a company's information.

In fact, the opposite is often true.

When you move your content out into the world where it can be found, commented on, and improved by those who need it and use it, it's not a competitive threat, it's a competitive advantage.

As discussed earlier in this book, collaboration is often the key to achieving results that are greater than the sum of the efforts of individual participants. When it comes to products, the people who know the most are often your customers. Particularly in the world of software, although it applies to other products as well, it doesn't matter how many scenarios you design and test for; your customers will find ways to use your product that you never thought of. They use your products regularly, and they will find both faults and new uses. They are creating information that is invaluable to you and your other customers.

The concept of user-generated content is neither new nor is it solely associated with the rise of social media, although the latter

---

[1] http://www.haynes.com/print

has helped bring the idea to more prominence in recent years. In fact, for the majority of human history this has been the normal way that information gets communicated. One person comes up with an idea, a thought, or a story, and as it is repeated, each teller adds his or her own contribution. The tradition of oral knowledge sharing is an ancient one that readily accepts the axiom that the community will add and embellish to the benefit of all. (See my presentation, "Why Publishing is No Longer the Last Step,"[2] for more on these ideas.)

The modern belief in the sanctity and veracity of the written word is a relatively product of 19th and early 20th century thinking.

In the early days of written communication, prior to the development of the printing press, texts were copied by hand, with each scribe adding commentary and input. Even in the early days of the printing press, print runs were small and changes were often made to manuscripts and texts between printings in reaction to social and political changes.

Even Shakespeare used customer feedback, plus input from other writers, in his work. What we now consider the definitive works are in fact just snapshots of a particular version of each play. Modern scholarship shows that Shakespeare would change parts of plays, often on a daily basis, reacting to audience feedback and events of the day. In many ways his works were "The Daily Show" of Elizabethan England. Shakespeare wrote for the stage and his audience, not for the written word and posterity. He was open to ideas from his customer base, and we should be, too.

---

[2] http://www.slideshare.net/webworks/why-publishing-is-no-longer-the-last-step-2513597

Within my two-decade career in technical and corporate communications, I have come across numerous examples of user generated content that pre-date web technology and social media.

One of my first jobs in the technical communication industry was writing repair documentation for the Concorde supersonic aircraft. At that point the aircraft was only operated by two airlines, British Airways and Air France, both of which had the authority to make engineering changes. As a result, it wasn't long before a British Airways Concorde differed significantly from an Air France Concorde. As we maintained and wrote the documentation for both airlines, they would submit the changes and we would put them into the manual, flagged as what we termed a COC (Customer Originated Change). Some pages would carry a British Airways masthead and others an Air France masthead. This was user-generated content, it just took time for it to be incorporated into the final product.

With modern Internet-based technology this basic idea of accommodating user-generated feedback has been made more explicit, and the speed of incorporation has increased to the point where it can be, but doesn't have to be, instantaneous.

The myth of inaccuracy

Another of the great myths about Internet-based feedback on content posted on open platforms, such as a wiki or a forum, is that because anyone can contribute they will be inaccurate.

Firstly, "anyone" doesn't really mean "everyone." You decide who can contribute, and how they can contribute. So, you can limit access to those you trust. However, be aware that as you tighten access you may end up with just the opinions of a small number of contributors, and you won't be able to harvest the collective knowledge and experience of the community.

If you are going to lock your content down so tightly that only a privileged few can contribute and no one can comment, then you may as well just set up a traditional static website or even produce a printed (or PDF) version of your information. However, if you don't want anyone to contribute to your content, but you do want a mechanism for encouraging and harvesting feedback, then a tightly controlled environment may still add value.

It may seem natural to assume that the larger the pool of contributors, the greater the opportunity for inaccuracy. Yet a 2005 study by the academic magazine Nature, cited by Stewart Mader in *Wikipatterns*[9], showed that the most open platform wiki, Wikipedia, is no less accurate than the Encyclopedia Britannica, and that when mistakes do occur they are corrected much more quickly. In open forums, with larger communities, people with particular areas of interest monitor and review the pages that match their own areas of expertise and fix mistakes quickly.

Defining user-generated content

When setting up your community content platform you need to consider what sort of user-generated content you want. Do you want to let members of your community add new content, edit existing content, or just comment on content? Or do you want to give various combinations of these privileges to different groups of users?

These decisions and privileges may differ from subject to subject, section to section, and user to user within a particular platform. And, if you have multiple community platforms such as wikis, forums, social network pages, etc., you may want to set different permission patterns for different communities.

Here are four basic levels of permission that you can consider:

- **Create New Content** – This is a great way to discover gaps in your information model. However, you have to be aware that it is almost inevitable that you will get duplicate content.

- **Edit Existing Content** – This is one of the most valuable aspects of having an open content platform. After all, in many ways it is the whole purpose. You need to consider how you will review and manage that content. (See the next section for more on this subject.)

- **Add comments** – Users can add separate comments, but cannot edit the contents. Locking users into a comment-only mode can be useful when you have "approved" content that must never be changed, such as legal disclaimers, safety notices etc. This is the most common process used for capturing user generated content.

- **Delete Content** – This privilege is something that would normally only be given to a system administrator, and it should be used with great caution. Often it is better to delete or move the content, but leave a note explaining why the content has been moved or deleted.

Managing the new content

In all of these cases you have to consider how you will monitor and control this user-generated information.

While it is true that there are no pre-existing rules on how you should set up and use a community platform, it is up to you and your users to develop a series of policies, procedures, and best practices that work for your platform(s).

In a corporate environment, you will most likely need some sort of editorial review and approval process. You may need someone to monitor recent changes and interact with contributors. That same person may also need to be available to answer comments, make observations, etc.

In a more technical environment you may need someone who can review changes and comments for technical accuracy, relevancy, and other factors that might cause safety, liability, and warranty issues.

Managing content ownership

One thing you need to consider with user-generated content is who owns that content. Do you consider the information to be in the public domain, or does the fact that the user logged in imply permission for you to reuse their contribution? Will you add attribution to contributions? Is the information on your community content platform under something like a creative commons license?[3]

---

[3] http://creativecommons.org/

With an internal, company-restricted platform, none of these are really an issue because all information added will be created under the terms of a typical work-for-hire employment contract where creative work and intellectual property developed on company time is owned by the company.

But with a public-facing platform, especially one where you actively encourage user-generated content and comments, you need a policy regarding all of these issues before you make the platform live.

Whatever your reuse policy is, you need to state it on the platform's homepage or welcome screen so that potential contributors are informed before they apply for a login. One approach is to develop a set of Contributor Guidelines, a full Disclaimer, and a User Agreement.

For instance, Atlassian[4] software, the makers of the Confluence wiki platform has a section on their documentation wiki clearly labeled "Contributing to Confluence Documentation"[5] that outlines the steps and permissions needed before you can change or create information on the wiki.

Atlassian allows anyone to make changes to the developer documentation (API guides, plugin development, and gadget development), provided they have signed up for a wiki username and are logged in to the wiki.

But for changes to the product documentation, they ask that you first sign a Contributor License Agreement (CLA). The purpose of the agreement is to define the terms under which intellectual

---

[4] http://Atlassian.com

[5] http://confluence.atlassian.com/display/DOC/Contributing+to+the+Confluence+Documentation

property has been contributed to the Atlassian Documentation Wiki. It allows the company to defend the documentation wiki if a legal dispute occurs concerning the contributed content.

Atlassian also clearly states that its documentation is published under a Creative Commons "cc-by" license. This means that anyone can copy, distribute, and adapt the documentation provided they acknowledge the source. The cc-by license is shown in the footer of every page so that those who contribute to the documentation know that their contribution falls under the same copyright.

Before you start a community platform implementation, do some research into how people who have set up similar platforms have addressed this issue, and see if the solutions they have adopted will also work for you.

You should discuss different licensing options with your company's legal team to make sure you follow company guidelines and practices.

Incorporating feedback

So now that you have feedback, what do you want to do with it?

Once new text or changes to existing text have been approved, it is simply a case of making the revised content the current displayed content.

The bigger question revolves around comments. Do you just leave them attached to the content for all time, or do you systematically review, incorporate, and delete old comments?

One practical approach is the following:

- Monitor all comments and post a response to each so the person who posted the comment knows it has been read.

- Let people know that a comment or suggested change is being considered or has been approved for incorporation.

- For platforms that support multiple versions of a product (such as software), create a new space for each version of the product. Leave comments related to a specific version with that version's text. If a comment suggests something will be used in the next version, then make a note to that effect. In the next version's instance, post the original with the feedback incorporated and allow a new set of comments on that version.

Another approach is to use a "traffic light" system where each page or block of text has next to it a visual indicator or icon showing its approval status.

- New text that has yet to be approved has a "red light" icon

- User-contributed text that is under review or has not been verified has a "yellow light" icon

- Text that has either not been changed since initial issue or contains reviewed and tested user-generated content has a "green light" icon

This technique gives visitors a quick visual indication of the approval status of any information on the site.

Round-tripping

As more and more community platforms are deployed to share business content, especially technical documentation, an idea that has been gaining in popularity is the concept of round-tripping. In her book, *Conversation and Community*[4], Anne Gentle defines round-tripping as "the conversion from source to (platform) and back."

This generally means taking your source content, converting it to the output needed for your platform of choice, collecting the changes made over a specific period of time, and incorporating them back into the source files before starting another round of editing and publishing.[6]

For most companies that have documentation wikis, this is currently done as a manual process. When I hear people using the phrase round-tripping they tend to be talking in terms of automating the process. When I have asked people what the business case is for implementing automated round-tripping, very few have an answer beyond "well it would be cool."

One notable exception where automated round tripping may be of benefit is with a multilingual platform. For instance, I recently heard about a wiki with a community base of 90,000 users that had copies of the base English wiki in twenty-two other languages. To ensure a true global reach the community had no requirement that members speak English to have access to the wiki. In this instance, round tripping would have to be coordinated with language translation memory systems to ensure a simultaneous update. A daunting task, but one that would have a measurable impact.

---

[6] True round-tripping between systems with different markup (e.g., between a wiki and XML) is hard to do because you have to capture every important aspect of each representation in the other representation, and then preserve those aspects as you convert both ways. Anyone who has tried a round-trip translation (for example, translating from English to Russian and then back again) has seen this problem.

If you think that you need round-tripping between the public content on your community platform and your source documents, think carefully about what you really need. Consider if there are any consequences to altering the source material. There may be legal and liability issues related to such changes. Going back to my days in aerospace documentation, in the unfortunate instance of an aircraft accident, all the work on the documentation was frozen, and we had to be able to reproduce the exact version of the documentation that was used the last time that particular aircraft was serviced. If you had automatic round-tripping of user-generated content into the source content, satisfying such a request would require your platform management and control systems to be synchronized with your document management and content version control systems.

It might seem that the best way to approach round-tripping is to develop a scripted, automated system to incorporate feedback and changes into the source content. However, this approach is also fraught with potentially harmful consequences. Without checks and balances you may overwrite sensitive information and potentially cause liability, safety, and warranty issues.

If the end result of round-tripping is important to you, and you do not want to go through the manual process of incorporating feedback and customer changes into the source content, you might consider using the platform itself as the new source for any changes after the initial publication cycle. That is, use the community platform as your authoring environment.

If you cannot use the platform itself as a content authoring environment – perhaps because you need to leverage the efficiencies, knowledge, and investment in existing authoring tools, or you need to create high-quality output alongside the platform from a single content source – then round-tripping may be an essential part of your process.

In such instances, you need to make sure that your process still includes what I term the "human element." No matter how much you manage to automate, you still need to include a person in the process who can ensure that all content coming from the community platform is appropriate, has been reviewed, and (if necessary) approved. This person also needs to ensure that the new content is correctly attributed and does not overwrite sensitive information.

Independent user content

No matter how you look at it, user-generated content is the new paradigm. People expect to be able to contribute. Social media has shifted the way we communicate with customers and the way customers communicate with you. People expect to be able to comment on, tag, and share information they find online.

But, the new communications model isn't just about letting customers comment on your content, it's also about listening. No matter what you do, or don't do, to facilitate conversation with your customers, they will create their own content about you and your products that you may not be aware off. Think about my niece's "awesome dude." Places like YouTube are full of independently produced content. The same is true of the multitude of online forums, email groups, blogs, etc. People are happy to share their knowledge with others, especially if it shows that they know more, or are smarter than, the company that produces the product.

You need to be listening and watching for such independent content. In fact you can encourage and reward it. People who spend time creating content about you and your products, even negative content, are already emotionally invested in what you do. They care, especially the ones who post negative comments, and you need to respond to that.

If someone takes the time to create some independent content that is useful, acknowledge it. Maybe offer to incorporate it in your official content with some sort of acknowledgement. If you foster a sense of ownership and contribution, then your customers can be your most effective sales force. Nothing works better than peer recommendation.

If your find negative comments, or content that isn't in line with your own policies and procedures for your products, then post positive responses correcting misunderstandings or misinformation. Don't be defensive and don't get into an on-line argument. Be factual, be polite, and offer to assist with the problem that initiated the post or comment.

You may find that your users are also ahead of you in the technology they use to create information. If you find that your customers are using media such as annotated graphics, animation, or user produced videos to explain things and ideas, while you are still delivering print, PDF, or static text based web-pages, then look at why they have chosen that media. Does it deliver your message better than you do? Independent customer-generated content can often be a pointer to exactly how your customers use your products, rather than the way you think they do.

Facilitate the creation and compilation of user generated content and everyone benefits. Don't fight it, embrace it.

13

The Technology Question

All those cables dangling behind your TV can be a real pain, but what's worse is finding that you can't connect them. As I mentioned earlier, I recently purchased a Roku and a Blu-Ray player. They both came with HDMI cables, which would have been great, except my flat-screen HD TV is nearly a decade old and was manufactured before HDMI was a standard (that word again) interface. So, I couldn't use the cables and instead had to jerry-rig a way to connect them, a work around that meant losing another component out of my stack of audio-visual goodies. I had to sacrifice one piece of longstanding functionality to accommodate two new ones; all because I'm a technology geek.

I love new technology, and I guess I'm what's now termed an early adopter. I had one of the first desk calculators (with reverse logic), several digital watches (whatever happened to them), and a Betamax VCR! Somehow I managed to avoid 8-track and laser-disc. These days I'm a bit more cautious in my technology purchases, but despite planning to wait for the iPad 2, I crumbled and bought a first generation iPad after a few months.

A friend of mine has a theory that the rapid changes in video technology are just part of a massive conspiracy to see how many times he will buy a copy of *Goldfinger*. As a fellow James Bond aficionado and scholar,[1] I know what he means.[2]

While such devotion to technology can lead to frustrations and occasional headaches when it comes to home entertainment systems, it can have serious impacts in a business environment, especially when developing a holistic view of your content.

---

[1] I am also the author of two books on James Bond: *JAMES BOND: The History of the Illustrated 007*[14] and *THE JAMES BOND LEXICON*[16]

[2] To date, copies of the movie Goldfinger have been available as Super-8mm projector tapes, Betamax and VHS video tapes, laser-disc, DVD, online streaming, and coming soon, Blu-Ray.

You need to remain above the technology. In his introduction to my book on wikis, *WIKI: Grow Your Own for Fun and Profit*[15], content strategist Scott Abel warns about the dangers of becoming addicted to software:

> The first step, as 12 step programs have touted for decades, is to admit you have a problem. Most organizations go about tackling content challenges by starting from the wrong vantage point. They don't start with the problem, they start by jumping toward what they believe is the solution – software. It's only natural. We've been programmed to think that software solves problems, when in reality, software introduces as many problems as it helps us to solve... especially, when you select the wrong software tool for the job.
>
> Avoiding the tool trap is easy. The first step is to admit you are addicted to software and that your addiction, like all addictions, can cause you to make decisions that may have very negative consequences. Don't allow yourself to start talking about software tools until you understand what your real challenges are. What problems are you trying to solve? Why are they problems? What do those problems cost your organization? And, what are you willing to do to make those problems go away?

This is a sentiment I prefer to summarize as:

> People, Culture, Sociology, Process, and
> Solutions first – Systems last.

Do not implement technology just for technology's sake. No matter how cool it appears, there should be a business need driving the requirement for that particular technology. Technology should be applied to solve problems or build opportunity. The application of unsuitable technology can cause way more problems than it solves.

Business needs must come before engineering and IT needs. First, define the business problems (content strategy / content management / content development) and then consider how to apply engineering and IT solutions to solve them. When you look at the business needs, also look at what you are doing with your current tools and technology. More often than not you will find you are doing things the same way just because of existing technology, systems, or tool constraints.

For instance I had a client who insisted that a particular type of graphic had to be below a certain file size. The problem was that this file size resulted in poor quality graphics. When asked where the requirement came from, the response was that the users of his online system expected graphics to load within a certain time, and this was the size of graphic that meet that requirement.

Now, fine tuning system behavior to match established user expectations is a good business practice. But even when it was shown that graphics of a much larger size and increased quality would load within the time constraints, the client insisted that the limited file size was needed to enable their production process to work efficiently. In fact they had several steps in the process just to convert and reduce graphics to this particular format and size. After several weeks of discussion and investigation, we were able to trace this requirement to a graphics tool that hadn't been used for several years, yet that file size limit had stuck as part of their process. With no change in the tool set, we were able to remove several steps in the production process, and the client started delivering higher quality graphics to his customers.

Figure out what you need to do, then find solutions that help you deliver on those needs. Once you have identified a need, how do you go about choosing what technology to apply? First look at what you already have. Don't rush into buying new tool sets if you can develop a migration strategy using your existing tools that will help manage change. Or maybe develop a phased approach of developing small changes with existing tools that bring short term gains, while transitioning to new tools over a period of time. However, you also need to avoid trying to force-fit existing tools onto a new process they weren't designed to support. That can quickly lead to a dead-end process, which may have a short term gain, but has no means to bring long term benefit.

If, and when, you make the decision to introduce new tools and technologies, be aware that your short term costs will inevitably go up and must be off-set by long term savings, efficiencies, and revenue opportunities. There will be a period of training, adjustment, and even a few dead-ends, which need to be identified and corrected. You need to look at and compare total costs of operation and ownership over a given period of time. The cost of introducing new technology and tools is about more than the purchase price. For example, there is a human cost, and not just in training. It may be that new tools and processes will require people with a completely different skill set than the ones you traditionally have on staff.

If you do decide that you need to change a tool set, look at what other people in your community and industry are doing and talking about. Research technology as much as you research the business issues. When you do make technology decisions, make sure that whatever you do is both scalable and, perhaps more importantly, transferable. Make sure that new tools and solutions are standards based. Have an exit strategy for your content.

Choosing different tools

As discussed above, leveraging existing tools can save money in the short term, but if you are going to go that route, make sure those tools give you a platform for the future. If so, great! If not, make sure you plan for the future, too. If you can't afford new tools now, then develop a migration strategy towards a scalable, transportable data set. This can be as simple as changing the way you author content in the existing tools.

For example, you might move from an unstructured to a structured authoring model or start using standard templates. The more you do to add intelligence to your content the better, and you can make a good start without investing in new tools.

However, if you want to get the most benefit from this sort of approach, you may need to investment in new tools and technology.

Planning for future technology

A significant part of planning for the introduction of new tools and technology is planning for the future. The problem is that nobody really knows what's coming next. In fact, given today's rapid development of communications technology, it's more difficult than ever to anticipate how your content is going to be produced and consumed.

A few days ago I was going through some old magazines (paper ones – remember those?) in my office and came across an article written by a technology futurist on what would be the ultimate cell phone of the future. It would allow you to connect to the Internet, play your digital music files, let you watch TV on the move, take photographs, and have voice recognition – In short, he was describing the iPhone 4. But the article was only written in 2005, just seven years ago, when what I have sitting on the desk next to me today still seemed like science fiction.

And who knows what's coming next. One area of potential content delivery that I'm actively involved with at the moment is the use of 3D rotatable graphics; in particular, the potential for taking engineering developed computer-aided design models and using them to deliver service information; maybe even having them animated so you could show how objects can be disassembled or assembled in real time in a language-independent format.

The industry groups I work with are already talking about how this can be extended to work with the emerging Augmented Reality applications that allow you to place virtual objects on top of real objects through cell phone cameras or special glasses. Some clients I work with already have virtual reality labs to prototype their products. When I started in the aerospace industry we employed teams of specialist carpenters to build wooden mock-ups (and this was only the 1980s), now everything is tested in a digital environment.

And what's coming after that? Some sort of biotechnology that will lead to Star Trek style isolinear chips? We've already passed the original Star Trek series' flip communicators and the Next Generation-style iPads. How about a Matrix plug-in so we can learn kung-fu in seconds? OK, maybe that one won't be such a good idea, but there are already some people testing implanted micro-chips containing their medical records. How about holograms? Or, something we haven't even conceived of yet?

The point is that unlike the days when an aerospace company could keep a team of carpenters employed for decades, we are now at the point where technology changes faster than business needs and processes, and you need to be positioned to move your content, and refine your process, from technology to technology.

Given this, it's reasonable to ask if there is any way to totally future-proof your content. The answer is no, at least not with a 100% certainty. However, you can mitigate a lot of the risk by using processes that are built on an open, standards-based architecture rather than proprietary tools, and, as mentioned previously, making sure you have a defined exit strategy for your content. Also, think beyond the media you use and consider the delivery mechanism: is your production process a closed one or is there a way to ensure that data can always flow in and out of it? The more distribution paths, the greater the opportunity to migrate your content to newer, alternative technologies.

Think about how difficult it would be for you today to retrieve something produced twenty years ago. Now project that scenario forward and think about someone in another twenty years having to access the content you are producing today – what can you do today that would make it easier for them to accomplish that?

Leveraging Your Content

14

Content as a
Revenue Source

A couple of years ago a friend of mine posted the following on his Twitter feed:

> OMG! (Company Name) actually charges for their owner's manuals! That's absurd.

Absurd? Really? Is that the common expectation – that all the manuals associated with a product should be "free"?

Over the years I have, at different times, worked with two companies that have almost identical, competing product lines. In general they each have around 50% of their given market (although actual market leadership tends to fluctuate between them on a year-to-year basis). Yet they have two diametrically opposed philosophies when it comes to supplying documentation.

Company A has the philosophy that when you buy their product, you get everything included to run, maintain, and operate it (but not to repair it), so they include the cost of producing the documentation in their product pricing. They make their money on spare parts.

Company B has the philosophy that when you buy their product, you just buy the product and then pay extra for the bits and services you need, as you need them, so they have a lower product price and charge for their documentation (and their spares too).

The total cost of ownership for both products over the normal operating span turns out to be just about the same.

Two scenarios

Let's take a look at the two scenarios in more detail.

Company A – Documentation included

This is perhaps considered the more traditional model. A content development team writes the manuals, help sets, etc., and publishes a complete suite of documentation. The whole suite is then delivered with the product. That suite can range from one small manual to literally (in the case of an aircraft) hundreds of large volumes. The cost of producing those manuals is covered in the product cost, and the customer perceives them as being "free."

Factoring in the cost of producing the content and distribution should be a given. In some companies I've worked with it is funded by a percentage of sales. However I've been amazed at the number of times that I've done consulting work for companies that don't even consider the cost of the documentation. They don't calculate it, they don't consider it a development cost, and they don't cover it in the price of their products.

Often companies like that consider documentation to be "a necessary evil" (a phrase I have heard more than once) and an uncontrolled overhead. As a result the content development is not considered an integral part of the design and production process and is poorly funded (if at all). The content producers are often isolated from the business process. The result is usually poor quality documentation.

As a general rule of thumb, if you buy a low-priced, commodity product and it includes "everything," then there is a fair chance that the associated content will be next to useless. (I know this is a broad stroke statement, and there are always exceptions to it).

Company B – Documentation separate

In this scenario, the cost of producing and distributing the product documentation is usually well understood and managed. Most products in this case will ship with a small "free" documentation set that covers the basics of getting started and simple operation (like the manual in your car's glove box, for instance) with the expectation that if customers want to know more, they are prepared to spend money.

Again, think of the car analogy – most people who want to maintain and repair their own cars will go and buy a book on how to do it. There are whole companies that write and sell specialist manuals for car dealers and repair shops. The vast majority of customers will never access a full documentation suite, so why provide it to everyone? The manufacturer can focus on producing the documentation that 80% of its customers need, and the other 20% can be covered by a recognizable revenue stream from selling the specialist content.

In cases like this, content development is often funded by a percentage of the additional revenue it supports (e.g., the sales of spares) or produces. This method of funding content development acts as an incentive to produce better quality content and, to use a sales term, includes a "call to action" that leads to more revenue opportunities.

One area where I believe the "pay as you need it" model breaks down is that, currently, most manuals you pay for (including the one that my friend was complaining about) are PDFs of traditional print manuals. You still end up buying the complete book even if you only want one or two sections of it.

If you have a pay-to-download model, why not break the manual into topics and use a system of micro-payments. Instead of asking customers to pay $10 (the amount that outraged my friend), $15, or $20, why not charge $0.99 a topic?

So which is the right approach? They both are. Whether or not you charge for documentation is a product of many factors, including the business plan, the content development team's role in your organization, customer expectations, etc. However, one underlying thing that applies is that the cost of documentation development should be correctly calculated and factored into the product development costs. You need to recoup those costs somewhere – it is simply a matter of deciding where in the product life cycle and how.

BUT... if I had to favor one, I'd say go the separate charge route. It gives you more flexibility for delivery, it gives the customer choice, it lowers product prices, and it turns the content development team from being an overhead into a profit center.

On a personal note, when I switched one documentation department from being overhead to being a revenue generator, it completely changed the way the role of documentation and the people who produced it were perceived.

And the customers liked it too.

When thinking about how your content can be a revenue generator, it's a great help if you just bear in mind that every company, no matter its size, is a publisher. Maybe not in the traditional sense of publishing books, but in the broader sense of publishing information. Having said that, the largest book publisher in the US, in terms of paper based products, is not Random House, or McGraw-Hill etc, but the US Government, with companies such as Boeing not far behind.

Again it's worth taking a look at the dictionary definition:[1]

pub·lish [transitive verb]

1. a. *to make generally known*
   b. *to make public announcement of*
2. a. *to disseminate to the public*
   b. *to produce or release for distribution*

Nearly every piece of content you produce in an organization falls into one or more of these categories, be it technical manuals, training materials, websites, marketing materials, sales proposals, statements of work, financial statements, internal policies and procedures, design documents, etc. If you start to think like a publisher, you can start to recognize new revenue opportunities.

- What content now being produced in your organization might be useful enough to your vendors, partners, and customers that they would be willing to pay for it?

- Do you need to deliver everything in great big manuals? How about smaller chunks of content at lower prices that allow more flexibility for you and your customers?

- Do you have existing content that can be repackaged and presented in new ways to your customers?

- Do your content distribution models fit your market and its expectations? Think about the impact of eBooks on the traditional publishing market. Are you prepared to take advantage of new technologies to leverage your content?

Begin to think outside the box about your content. Stop thinking about it as a "necessary evil" or an overhead. Start thinking about

---

[1] http://merriam-webster.com/dictionary/publish

it as a product in the same way an equipment manufacturer thinks about spare parts. People will pay for knowledge and information, so make sure you give them the opportunity to do that.

It is true that in today's Internet economy you may have to give away certain information that you previously charged for, but that can lead to several advantages:

- It can position you and your company as thought leaders in a particular niche or industry space.

- Having information publicly available can reduce the costs of sales and support. It can even provide sales leads. In short it is a very effective marketing tool.

- If you give some information away for free, people are more prepared to pay a premium for the more detailed specific content that they need.

Indirect revenue impacts.

Content revenue may not always come from a direct sale, but it can have a significant impact on the bottom line through other means. For instance, many large equipment manufacturers make higher profits from service and parts than from selling the equipment itself. Even a small improvement in content quality can mean more efficient parts ordering and have a significant impact on revenue.

Or consider the recent case of United Airlines, which estimates that switching from paper flight manuals to electronic ones on tablet computers will save 16 million sheets of paper and 326,000 gallons of jet fuel per year.[2]

---

[2] http://www.marketwatch.com/story/united-airlines-launches-paperless-flight-deck-with-ipad-2011-08-23

Or the major construction company that, by building a library of common terms and templates for its bid proposals, improved the quality of its responses, which resulted in them closing at least 6% more bids and earning approximately $1 Billion in additional revenue![3]

Now that's a significant impact on the bottom line, no matter which way you look at it.

---

[3] Joe Gollner presentation at LavaCon 2011.

15

Quality Content

I subscribe to several email lists about various aspects of business writing and communication. Most days I just skim through, occasionally speed reading the odd post. About once a month I consider unsubscribing, but then something like this pops up:

> We still use process X, and while we (the tech writers) think it is useful, I think our users mostly rely on process Y to achieve the same result. We've attempted to educate our users on the value of our way of doing things, but based on the questions I get, I don't think a lot of our users think of using process X on a regular basis.

Wow – so if I get this straight, the users of the information like to use it one way (Y), but the content creators think they should be using it another way (X) so they make every effort to "educate the users" as to how it should be done. If the majority of the people who use your content are following the same behavior pattern, isn't it better to look at why they are doing that and the value that THEY find rather than the value that YOU think is there.

Learn from your customers. Find out why they prefer Y to X, and then do what you can to make Y even better. If that means dropping process X, then do so. Those of you who have heard me talk will have heard this before: the documentation industry is not about us as content creators, it's about our customers and how they access, assimilate, and use that content.

Good content can both answer questions and move prospects along the sales pipeline, reducing cycles and costs of sales. People looking to find out about you and your products will find your content before they ever talk to a sales person.

First impressions do last.

Put yourself in the place of your customer or prospect. What do people want to know about you, your products, and your services?

I was having a conversation the other day with a friend of mine about how, as he put it, "restaurant websites are stuck in the nineties." We were planning to go out for a dinner with our wives and were looking for a new place to eat. It rapidly became an exercise in frustration. Nearly every website we looked at hadn't been updated in years and mostly consisted of static webpages loaded with irrelevant marketing blurb. I often hear restaurant websites cited as the prime examples of poor website design. Why is that?

Because they like to lead with how they are "a unique dining experience," or something similar, when the truth is that the majority of people looking at restaurant websites want to know two things, your location and when you are open. That's closely followed by phone numbers for reservations and the menu. So why lead with how pretty the dining room looks?

So what is good content?

Simply put, good content should do at least one, and preferably a combination, of the following three things:

1. Answer questions
2. Inform
3. Add value

Answer questions

This may seem obvious, but as discussed before, too often content presented to customers is all about what something does, when in the vast majority of cases customers want to know how to do something. Do you know what questions your customers ask the most?

I remember at one company, I was asked to create the Frequently Asked Questions section for the website. So I asked if they had a list of the FAQs that came in to sales, support, or over the phone. "Oh, just come up with something yourself" was the answer, "we don't track stuff like that." What I produced wasn't really a page of FAQs, it was more a page of "Things that Alan thinks might be frequently asked questions based on his experience with the product." – TTATMBFAQBOHEWTP – Not really as catchy is it?

And, have you noticed that FAQ pages are often buried away deep within a website structure. Why is that? If there are frequent-asked questions, the answers should be front and center and easy to find. In fact, to my mind no website should have a FAQ page. The whole website should be designed around answering those questions in an intuitive way.

This philosophy doesn't just apply to websites. Think about the FAQs for all the content that you produce and distribute. Are you answering those questions? Do you in fact even know what those questions are?

Inform

Again this should seem obvious, but it is worth remembering one of the first rules of writing, which also applies to any form of business-related content creation: know your audience. Present them with relevant information that they can process. I recently did a survey of a website that was aimed at a target group of customers, most of whom would be non-native English speakers, and while the content was relevant, most of it was written at a college graduate reading level, making it inaccessible to the target audience.

I have also seen many examples of content that restates the obvious and is even patronizing to the content consumers. When this happens, people quickly become irritated and stop using the content.

Developing content that delivers information and informs the right audience in the right way is a difficult balancing act.

Add value

I originally titled this section, "impart knowledge," but that misses an important point. The right answer needs to add value that helps your customer achieve some objective, not just provide some knowledge.

That objective can be as simple as finding a phone number to something as complex as finding the procedure to disassemble a piece of equipment or code a computer program. Or, it could be gaining background information on a topic of interest. To add value, you may need to provide information in a format that gives a better sense of place and context, for instance showing a disassembly procedure as a 3D animation rather than as a series of static 2D illustrations.

Whatever it is, good content makes the content consumer feel satisfied and fulfilled.

Mamet's three rules

There is a famous memo from writer/producer David Mamet to his writing staff on a TV show[1] that boils down the essence of dramatic writing to three questions :

1. Who wants what?
2. What happens if they don't get it?
3. Why now?

These three questions also apply to content creation in business.

- **Who wants what?** What information do your customers, partners, employees, etc. need?

- **What happens if they don't get it?** Lost sales, broken products, dissatisfied customers, missed business opportunities, increased costs, etc.

- **Why now?** What factors result in a particular person needing a particular piece of content at any given time.

Unhappy customers

Good content will mean happy customers, and happy customers will talk about you. But so will unhappy customers. In fact they are more likely to talk about you than the happy ones. One of the most enlightening statements I ever heard about customer relations was that unhappy customers are often the most invested in you and your products. They generally want you to succeed and are expressing disappointment, and frustration, more than

---

[1] The full text of Mamet's memo can be found at http://movieline.com/2010/03/-david-mamets-memo-to-the-writers-of-the-unit.php

anger. The fact that they are taking the time and energy to post feedback, albeit negative, is an indication of that investment.

If your content results in unhappy customers, and this will sometimes happen, you need a non-confrontational strategy for engaging with them, discussing their issues, and above all resolving their issues. If you engage them, and resolve their issues, in my experience they will often turn around and become your strongest product champions.

The customer experience

There is no marketing cure for sucking, the last thing you want to do is ignore the customer experience.
—Elyse Tager, Constant Contact

Make sure you allow your customers to interact with your content and with each other. This can be through social platforms such as wikis, social networks, message boards, forums, or even mailing lists. If you don't, someone else will.

You also need to regularly act like your customer acts. Do the things that your customer needs to do. Even better, get a friend or family member who has no knowledge of your company's culture and process to try and use your content to achieve a specific task and give you feedback. This could be things like ordering a part from your service information systems, finding a phone number, trying to get the answer to a simple question, or calling the support line. Even just calling the office to see what the phone system message says can be useful.

Above all don't take your content and process for granted, and don't take your content customers for granted.

16

Finding Things

I'm sure this, or something similar, has happened to you. A few years back, in the days when I used to compete in the occasional Autocross competitive driving event with my MINI Cooper S, I attended a performance driving school. During the day's event, the instructor suggested that my driving style would suit a particular brand of tire, different from the one I was currently using. Great, I thought, I'll get a set for the upcoming season.

The instructor had given me both the manufacturer and tire type name, so I thought it would just be a case of going to the website. Oh no, it wasn't going to be that easy. A search on manufacturer's website came up with an "item not found" message. So I tried looking under "racing tires" – no luck. So I typed in the size of tire I needed. Nothing. I spent a frustrating afternoon trying to find and order these (not inexpensive) tires. In the end I gave up and ordered my usual brand with two clicks on that manufacturer's web-site, and even arranged to have them delivered to a tire store near my house so I could get them mounted on my racing wheels.

A few days later I found out on one of the drivers' forums that the manufacturer of the recommended tires had changed their product line and was now offering them under a new brand and model name, which meant having to order them from a completely different web-site!

The simple fact is that no matter what job, hobby, or profession we are in, we tend to spend an inordinate amount of time just looking stuff up. In fact in its 2010 report *Mobility in Service*[1], the Aberdeen Group stated that "Currently the average service firm reports a 56% utilization." That means that nearly half a day is spent in non-productive tasks, prime among which is looking up information so they can carry out the service tasks they get paid for.

The truth is that the answers that people are looking for are often there, but simply can't be found. Designing, developing, and delivering your content in a way that helps people find the answer they need intuitively, quickly, and easily will give you an immediate competitive advantage. Customers will return, again and again, to companies that give them the information they need when they need it.

The more that people come to you because you know how to answer their questions, and can deliver content that helps them, the more you will be seen as a thought leader. One of the best compliments I've ever been paid by a client was to be told "You have answers in situations when other people only have questions." That's a great objective to aim for when it comes to presenting your content.

It's a truism that if you don't get your content right, it doesn't matter what else you ship. Also, it doesn't matter how "slick" the delivery platform is if the content isn't right. An iPad won't make up for poor content.

When defining how you want to deliver good content to your customers, you have to balance business needs with thinking like a customer.

From a business perspective, what is it that drives revenue? For instance, as an equipment manufacturer that sells spare parts, do you want to design and deliver content that makes it easier for the customer to find and order the correct parts? Think about what costs you want to reduce. As a software company, are you spending too long dealing with support calls?

Think about what's important from the customer perspective. For example, airlines really only make money when an aircraft is in the air, time on the ground costs money. Can you design and deliver content that helps reduce loading or maintenance times? Software companies need their products to keep working. A colleague of mine used to call this a "software dial tone" and developed a way of delivering network status updates using a graphical interface.

Another way to think about how you deliver content is to think of your customer in terms of a Hollywood movie. Now, I'm not suggesting that you should visualize all your customers as looking like George Clooney, or Nicole Kidman; I'm thinking more in terms of story structure.

Towards the end of several of the various conference presentations I've given in recent years I have a slide that mentions several recommended books as "must reads." One of them is Robert McKee's STORY: Substance, Structure, Style and the Principles of Screenwriting[11].

Anyone who has heard me speak or read my blog[1] will know that I'm a strong advocate of storytelling in all forms of communication. I believe it applies as much to business content and communication as it does to your favorite novel or movie. Picking up on that thought, I decided to see if I could apply McKee's 10 Commandments of Storytelling to business content.

1. **Thou shalt not take the crisis or climax out of the protagonist's hands.**

   So who is the "protagonist" of your content? It could be your product, but the most likely candidate is that your "protagonist" is the person using your content. Your content should be produced in such a way that your protagonists can use the information so that they feel that they have solved the

---

[1] http://thecontentpool.com

crisis (or put more prosaically, overcome the problem) themselves based on the knowledge you have presented. Another storytelling trick, often cited by screen-writer Todd Alcott, is to ask yourself, "What does the protagonist want?"

2. **Thou shalt not make life easy for the protagonist.**

This seems contrary to the very purpose of content developed to help a customer. Isn't it our job to make life easier? Yes it is. But in certain types of content, such as training materials, you may want to include challenges and then guide the reader through them.

This way you can build a sense of accomplishment as the reader progresses through the material. A recent trend is the "gamification" of content, i.e., applying the concept of game theory to entice users to read and absorb the intent of the content.

3. **Thou shalt not use false mystery or surprise.**

Don't hold back anything that is integral to full understanding of the product or service you are developing content about. But, also make sure to reveal information in a logical manner that is considerate of you readers' needs. Make sure they have the information they need, when they need it.

4. **Thou shalt respect thine audience.**

The first rule of any sort of writing is "know your audience." Know them and respect their level of knowledge. If you are developing content for experts, then you may not need to include the basic information that you might use for a more general consumer market. You can use conditional tags to serve different topics and statements to different audiences, based on their background, within a common set of content.

5. **Thou shalt have a god-like knowledge of your universe.**

A joke I often use is, "What's the definition of an 'expert'?" The answer is, "it's a person who has read two more pages in the manual than you have." So what does that make the person who wrote the manual in the first place? We may not know everything about what we are creating content for, but we should give the reader the confidence that we do.

6. **Thou shall use complexity rather than complication.**

Most of what we write about in business, and especially in technology based industries, is by its very nature, complex. We should take that complexity and break it down into logical steps and topics that can guide the reader. We should never use complexity as an excuse for making the content complicated.

7. **Thou shalt take your character to the end of the line.**

We learn in grade school that every story should have a beginning, a middle, and an end. The same applies to business content too. The narrative should guide the reader through the process, or information, in such a way that it flows logically and that at the end they know more, or have achieved more, than when they started.

8. **Thou shalt not write "on the nose" dialog.**

Wait, I hear you asking, there's no dialog in business content so how does this apply? Well the definition of "on the nose dialog" relates to the scene when a character says, aloud, exactly what he is thinking or describes what is happening around him. So how does this apply to business content? Do you have sections of content that restate the obvious? Try reading your content out aloud? Is it boring and repetitious?

In textual content try altering sentence lengths. Don't think anyone ever listens to technical content as if it was dialog? As a teenager I spent hours working under cars while a buddy nearby would read the steps from the manual for me to follow. How about a visually impaired customer using a reading device?

9. **Thou shalt dramatize thine exposition.**

Put simply, "show don't tell." In prose or on the screen this means have your characters reacting to an event, not talking about it. But isn't our job to tell people how to do something? Yes it is, but the key word is "how."

Replace long descriptive texts on operational theory with a few active steps users can take that demonstrate the product, and they will gain a quicker understanding. People learn more by doing than they do by being told.

10. **Thou shalt rewrite.**

Do I need to explain this one? Plan your schedule to include time to develop, review, and revise your content. The best of all scenarios is to develop the content, do a quality/feasibility check by having someone actually use your draft to accomplish the tasks you have written about, and ask for feedback.

Better yet, watch them try to use your content. Then go back and revise based on your observations. They say that any good piece of art is never finished. Content development is art, even business and technical content. You can always improve on what you've done.

Content is not just the formal stuff that you distribute in manuals or post to your website. It encompasses every aspect of communication, both inside and outside the company. Content can be be anything that engages the senses:

- Text
- Graphics
- Sound
- Video / Animation
- Color

Color is one aspect of content design and development that is often overlooked and can also have unforeseen cost implications. Many years ago I worked for a company that was, along with two others, merged to form a brand new company. The CEO of the new company helped design the logo and picked the new corporate colors. He insisted on a particular shade of green for one part of the logo. The problem was the particular shade of green he wanted wasn't a Pantone color.[2] As a result, every printed item in the company had to be special-ordered, from business cards to special letterhead paper – in short it cost a fortune!

Depending on your target audience, color blindness can be an issue. Up to 20% of males exhibit some degree of color blindness, while fewer than 0.5% of women do. If this is a potential issue, and it probably is, make sure that you use combinations of position, shape, and color, rather than relying on only color when you need to convey a distinction. This can be as simple as using the color in a consistent manner and place. For instance, although color-blind people may not see a red traffic light as red (well not red as the majority of the population perceives it), they still know that the top light on a traffic light stack means "Stop."

---

[2] Pantone colors are a printing industry color standard (there's that word again).

Sound is important too. Think about the greeting message on your voice mail or even what you play when someone is on hold. Ever hung up because the hold music is tinny, grating, or even worse plugged into some local radio station where you end up listening to a babbling DJ? Every customer interaction is an opportunity to present good quality content. "Your call is important to us" and "The menu has recently changed" don't count as good quality content.

Consider every touch point customers have with your company. What's the experience like? Does every step help move customers closer to answering their questions.

What's your communication strategy for dealing with customers? How will your content reflect that?

- Do you have specified response times?

- When does the communication become personalized?

- When do you switch media and approach? Is there a point where you move from email to the phone?

- What sort of language is being used? Is it loaded with jargon or acronyms that only someone inside your company would understand?

It's an easy thing to do and something that we are all guilty of. In many ways it's a natural, and maybe in some cases a desirable, side effect of effective communications. When we meet, communicate, and collaborate, we naturally develop a shared vocabulary and an underlying knowledge base within the group. This helps us communicate quickly and effectively without having to go back to basics. But when someone new joins the group, or more importantly, when the group needs to communicate outside its membership, these underlying common assumptions become barriers to communication. Even within the same company or industry, you can't assume that someone else knows what you know or has the same frame of reference.

Think about the underlying assumptions you are making about your customer base. Remember, they may not have easy access to the information that you think they do. For instance, one client I worked with had set up its online support website on the assumption that customers would know that the information was organized on the basis of product serial numbers. Yet analysis of the website showed that over 5,000 transactions a year started with customers trying to guess serial number prefixes (never mind the actual numbers). The addition of a home page with a "you need the serial number" message and a short "how to find the serial number" graphic had an immediate effect in increasing web site usage and reducing support calls.

You also need to think about the way you organize and group your content. The way that you organize information for design and manufacturing purposes is most likely different than the way your customers will expect to access it for maintenance, repair, and support needs.

"New improved..." a phrase we've all seen used in advertisements and on consumer product packaging inciting people to believe that they need the latest version of a product. But think about that phrase for a second. By saying your new product is improved, are you implicitly admitting that your previous product wasn't as good as it should be. And exactly how is it "improved?"

Subjective terminology of this type can cause potential issues in business communications and content development. In fact it can even lead to legal issues. Is your customer's interpretation of "better" the same as yours, or are you promising a new experience or level of service that your customer doesn't believe you are delivering?

While some subjective text may be useful in marketing campaigns (though I actually doubt that assertion), you should avoid it in all technical content, and examine any possibly subjective content for potential misinterpretation. If you use phrases, such as "bigger," "better," "acceptable," etc., that raise questions like "than what?" or "in what way?," look for objective ways to say the same thing.

No matter how much effort you put into creating great products, services, and content, there will always be someone at some point who is unhappy and is prepared to let you know about it. So how do you deal with complaints?

Complaints are actually the best opportunities for great customer support. People who complain are by nature engaged and passionate about you and your products. They have an underlying desire to see you succeed. The very fact that they have taken time to communicate with you, which is more than the vast majority of people who hit a problem do, shows that level of commitment. Engage with that commitment, go the extra step, make complainers feel that you are interested in their issues and that they have a degree of ownership in the resolution, and they can become your strongest advocates.

If you get a generic complaint such as "your documentation sucks" or "I can't find anything on your website," don't respond with an equally generic note. Instead, ask for more details, try to find out what, exactly, the customer was trying to use the documentation for, ask how it could be better organized, find out what the customer was looking for and what search terms were used, etc.

If you have public areas, such as user forums, message boards, social network accounts, or wikis, where people can leave negative comments, leave those comments in place and respond in a positive, helpful manner. Allow other people to see that you are engaged with your community. Leaving a negative comment unanswered is just as bad, and in some ways, worse than making a negative response.

Positive action to complaints can even be used to your advantage. In Austin, TX, we have local chain of movie theaters called The Alamo that has a very strict policy of throwing out people who talk and text during movies. This policy, along with fun and innovative programming, has made The Alamo a local favorite for serious movie goers. A few months ago they threw a young lady out for incessantly texting during a show. The following day she left a heated, and at times vitriolic, voice mail on the theater's phone system. The movie chain took the voice mail and used it as a soundtrack to a video explaining what the policy was and why they had it. Within days of posting the video it went viral and was soon being talked about, played on national TV, and spread all over the Internet. The underlying message and response from those who saw it was, "I wish my local movie theater did that too."

Which brings me to my last point. The Alamo video exposed the fact that a lot of moviegoers were unhappy at the level of service being offered by their local theaters. I don't know if any theater managers, or chain owners, saw that and altered their own policies in response, but they should have.

One of the quickest ways to find out if the content you are developing is along the right lines and meeting the needs of your market is to look at how your competitors' content and communications work.

Look at what's good and what's bad. Adapt one, learn from the other.

Yes, you need to differentiate yourself from the competition, but don't do it at the expense of the customer experience. In fact, the opportunity is to differentiate by developing and delivering exceptional content that will enhance the customer service experience.

17

Develop a Content Strategy

When I was growing up, my grandmother and I used to sit together most Saturday evenings to watch her favorite game show on the BBC, *The Generation Game*. The show consisted of four teams of two people from the same family, but from different generations, who competed to win a variety of prizes. It wasn't exactly the greatest TV or the most educational,[1] but it was something I shared with my grandmother.

One of the regulars on the show was a circus plate spinner, who would first demonstrate his skill and then invite the players to try and emulate his feat, with the inevitable smashing results. As a kid that was always my favorite segment, and it provided a metaphor I've used throughout my professional career.

Not long after I started in the content development profession, I was managing multiple projects, and the spinning plate analogy seemed particularly apt. I remember using it one day in a meeting, and a colleague with far more experience retorted with, "If you think it's difficult now, wait a few years – then it will be like trying to spin plates on the deck of a moving aircraft carrier!"

He was right. When I contemplate the start of a major content design, development, and distribution project these days, I inevitably see lots of moving parts operating in a constantly shifting environment. To be successful in such an environment, you need to manage the variables that keep things "spinning" and minimize the number and impact of the, inevitable, "breakages." In short you need a holistic view of your content across the enterprise and a strategy for dealing with it.

You need a content strategy to make sure it all works together.

---

[1] The show must have had something going for it because it originally ran from 1971 to 1982 and was revived for a second run between 1990 and 2002.

Defining content strategy

What do we mean by content strategy? The truth is that there is no one definition. Although many of us have been applying some of the ideas and concepts for a long time, the term and practice of content strategy is a relatively new discipline. It was first used in the 1990s in specific reference to the development of web sites, but it has come to mean a lot more. The term is now used across various disciplines such as user experience design, content management, business analysis, technical communications, and more.

A quick web search brings up several different definitions for content strategy, including:

- "Planning for the creation, publication, and governance of useful, usable content" – Kristina Halvorson, "The Discipline of Content Strategy"[6].

- "A repeatable system that defines the entire editorial content development process for a website development project." – Richard Sheffield, *The Web Content Strategist's Bible*[20].

- "Words and data to create unambiguous content that supports meaningful, interactive experiences." – Rachel Lovinger, "Content Strategy: The Philosophy of Data"[7].

- "A repeatable process or methodology that manages content within the entire content lifecycle." – Rahel Anne Bailie.[2]

They are all correct, and equally valid, within their own environment and context.

---

[2] http://knol.google.com/k/content-strategy

My hypothesis is that content strategy doesn't fit within these separate activities and definitions, but should be an over-arching concept that draws them together to achieve a common purpose.

My personal view of content strategy is perhaps most closely aligned with the statement that content strategy is about:[3]

> achieving business goals by maximizing the impact of content.

Many Fortune 500 companies now actively recruit and employ content strategists.[4] In fact, the Disney Corporation has had a formal content strategy practice for over ten years.

If you are just starting to consider a content strategy, you may want to hire an external consultant. Consultants, or at least the good ones, can provide an impartial extra pair of eyes and ask questions about how, and why, things are done without any underlying prejudices and influences. A good consultant should not accept the answer, "we've always done it that way," and should work with you to tie content design, development, and delivery decisions to your business needs.

When looking to hire an external consultant, remember that anyone can call themselves a content strategist. Make sure the person you are considering has a track record and a good industry reputation. And, perhaps most importantly, make sure that their vision and definition of content strategy is in alignment with yours.

---

[3] Paraphrased from "Content Strategists: What Do They Do?"[30] by Dan Zambonini.

[4] At the 2010 LavaCon conference in San Diego, one speaker declared content strategists as "the new corporate rock stars!"

The perspective a content strategist brings to an engagement can be strongly influenced by their training and professional background. Some will specialize in content analysis, some in web editorial guidelines and tools, yet others will consider themselves as information architects. A good content strategist will position themselves in a way to cover all these aspects, plus interact and collaborate with others such as programmers, visual designers, use experience specialists, copywriters, etc. A true content strategist will bring a holistic view to enabling you to leverage your content to meet your business needs.

As mentioned in Rahel Anne Bailie's quote above, content strategy is not just about defining a strategy about content creation; it's about Content Lifecycle Management. It is far more than an editorial process, or website design, or any one aspect; it's a full business process.

Bailie postulates that the content lifecycle is a four stage process:[5]

 ... the strategic analysis, the content collection, management of the content, and publishing, which includes publication and post-publication activities. The content lifecycle is in effect whether the content is controlled within a content management system or not, whether it gets translated or not, whether it gets deleted at the end of its life or revised and re-used.

You need to understand your content from creation to disposal. Knowing when content is obsolete is as important as knowing

---

[5] http://knol.google.com/k/content-strategy#

when to create it. Not only ask why a piece of content is needed, but also ask where does it fit, who is going to use it, and for how long will they use it.

Understand your content lifecycle. Map it. And know where individual pieces of content are on it.

It my seem obvious, but an essential part of your content strategy should be to make sure that you protect your intellectual property and make sure that you do in fact own the content that you think you own. Sharing your content and ideas is fine and can lead to greater benefit all around. (I covered the benefits of collaboration in Chapter 7, and in greater depth in *WIKI: Grow Your Own for Fun and Profit*[15]). But sharing should be beneficial to both parties. You need to know who owns what, and perhaps more importantly, who will have the rights to it in the future. Establish when content is owned and when it is licensed.

Just to give an example of how this can affect a business, I was involved in an industry project where a particular set of content had been given to the project by one of the participating companies. This content was then being used as the basis to develop a new industry-wide standard. Two years into the project it was revealed that the company that had donated the base content didn't actually have the rights to donate it. It had in fact been originally developed by another subsidiary company, which had only licensed it to the parent, donating company.

I have also heard stories of companies being sued because of the unapproved use of a customer's logo on their website. I have also seen a sales person instantly lose a potential sale because he used someone else's content in his PowerPoint presentation without permission.

Make sure that the content you are going to use is yours or that you have the right licenses and permissions to use it.

The ripple effect

One way to measure if you have an effective content strategy is, of course, to measure the impact of any changes on the business need you are addressing. However, this can sometimes take a long time, especially if you are embarking on an extensive, enterprise-wide realignment of how you design, develop, and distribute your content.

In such cases it is advisable to set interim goals and measure the success of improvements in line with these goals. This will generate a ripple effect as the improvements work their way across the enterprise.

For instance, the content strategy model below gives a path for this "ripple effect" moving across a large equipment manufacturing company whose ultimate business goal was to increase revenue through a more efficient and accurate spare parts ordering process.

Start with the *Content Creator*:

- Improve content creation processes.
- Introduce automation of repetitive tasks.
- Reduce Costs.
- Improve cycle times.

Move on to *downstream users* like Support and Training:

- Supply all-in-one consistent information resources.
- Accelerate product adoption.

- Reduce operating costs.

Deliver interactive product information on demand to *sales force, dealers, maintenance and repair groups*:

- Improve first time response and fix rates.
- Reduce errors.
- Increased effectiveness and efficiency.
- Enhanced customer satisfaction.
- Increased profits.

Deliver real-time targeted multi-channel content to *your customers*.

- Improved ordering accuracy.
- Increased revenues.
- Reduced support resolution times.
- Improved customer loyalty.

By mapping both the ultimate, and interim business goals across the enterprise, it's possible to develop a content strategy that provides almost immediate returns on investment.

Proven benefits of a content strategy

The following are just a few examples, from my own experience, of the sort of business benefits that can be achieved through the application of a well designed and implemented content strategy.

- **Pharmaceutical companies:** Faster creation and increased reuse of content leading to reduced costs and increased ability to share information between departments and laboratories.

Achieved full regulatory compliance. Doubled capacity without adding additional staff.

- **Biomedical equipment supplier:** 50% reduction in time spent to produce content.

- **Banking services company:** Improved speed of production, allowing for multichannel content distribution and introduction of personalized content delivery.

- **Software company:** Reduced support staff by 50%. Increased product release cycles from one a year to three a year.

- **Aerospace maintenance support company:** Took on three new aircraft types, a 30% load increase, with only 10% increase in staff.

- **Medical procedures company:** Reduced redundancy/duplication of content; product creation time cycle reduced by 67% or more.

- **Electronic payments network:** Twice yearly policy and procedure updates now rolled out at same time as software rather than delayed as had been the norm.

- **Maintenance training system:** Switched to 3D models with embedded animated instructions resulting in 25% savings in equipement maintenance and repair time in the field.

Keeping afloat in the Content Pool

Creating a content strategy isn't a one-off exercise. As with all business processes, it should be regularly reviewed and adjusted to reflect changing business needs, new markets, evolving technology, and external social factors. Developing a content strategy will help you build a path to navigate the Content Pool, and regular management and refining of that strategy to account for changing tides will help you stay afloat.

I hope that if there is one thing that has been clear over the preceding chapters is that there is a lot to think about when it comes to identifying, managing, and leveraging your content. Content is the intellectual life-blood of your organization, and it needs to be considered as a strategic assets. Other business assets of equivalent value (and it's possible to argue that there are, in fact, very few that match up to the value of your content), will undoubtedly have key business strategies, processes, goals, and key performance indicators assigned to them – it should be the same for your content.

18

The Case For A Chief Content Officer

As I mentioned at the conclusion of the previous chapter, your content is an asset worthy of the same attention, management, and visibility as any other strategic business asset, and as such there is a strong case that it should be managed at a senior executive level. However, being realistic, very few, if any, companies are going to leap immediately from undervaluing their content assets to having them overseen and cared for at the highest levels of the organizations.

First you need to take steps towards raising the profile of content design and development, deliver quality content, and prove its value to the organization.

Five ways to make executives love content development

"We never get any respect," is a refrain I've heard over and over again during my time in the content development industry. In fact I've even said it myself a few times. The refrain is often followed by, "no one really understands what we do, or the value we provide." The unfortunate thing is that in a lot of cases these refrains have some justification; but it needn't be that way.

Over the years I've visited hundreds of content development teams in a variety of companies and industries, but one of my most striking memories is the sheer contrast between two content development groups at a couple of luxury car manufacturers.

At the first company, the group in question had a nice modern office in a new campus setting. They had all the latest computers and access to great technology. In the parking lot outside the office was a fleet of not only their own cars, but those of their nearest competitor. Any member of the content team could use any of the cars in exchange for filling out a small usability report. The team was a high profile part of the customer support organization and were considered by the marketing team as a key part of the product "life style" branding activities.

At the second company, the comparable group worked in an old hut (in fact it was an old coal bunker) at the back of the factory, far removed from the production line, engineering, or any other function it needed to interact with. Although cars were parked outside, the team had no access to them. They had only a handful of computers, and their technology was at least five years behind their competitors. Their sole mandate was to produce a small, defined set of hardcopy manuals. And that's all they did.

So why the difference? In short the team at the first company acted like they were part of the company and projected a positive image of their skills. As such they were recognized and rewarded. The team at the second company stuck to the "we are only writers" approach. They were, in many ways, responsible for their own position.

So, if you feel that your content development team is "in the coal bunker," how do you change things so that you get the keys to the luxury cars?

The following presents a five-point action plan to help you raise the profile of what you do and make your executives realize your value.[1]

1. **Realize exactly what it is your team does:** Before you can raise your profile, you need to know what you have to offer.

---

[1] This section is based on an original post at TheContentPool.com blog http://-4jsgroup.blogspot.com/2009/06/5-ways-to-make-executives-love.html%7D

Chances are that most content development teams have talents and skills that exist nowhere else in the organization, and I'm not just talking about the ability to write. Also, most often the content development process is the only place in a company where all the company's intellectual property comes together. Content development isn't about "producing user manuals," it's about managing your organization's greatest asset – knowledge.

2. **Tell a good story:** People react to stories on an instinctive level. It's easier to remember stories than dry facts and figures. Content developers are the natural bridge between the end user and the company design, engineering, and production teams. Gather stories and tell them – repeatedly. Come up with your own stories that illustrate the importance, frequency, and impact of your own work. Develop fun trivia about what you do that people will remember and repeat.

3. **Offer your services for fun and profit:** Develop an in-house user community, not just an external one. Look around for other functions that you could work with or offer your expertise to. Develop an entrepreneurial mind-set and you will find opportunities to transform content development from an overhead cost-center into a profitable contributor.

4. **Hook an executive sponsor:** Find an executive's pet project that could use some creative input – maybe a little wordsmithing or some graphic design work – and get involved. While the work is progressing, make sure to bring that executive into your environment and show off what your team can achieve.

5. **Change attitudes:** If you go around say "I'm only a writer" or "publications never gets any respect," then people will believe you and act accordingly. Be aware of what you do and what

you can offer, and be proud of it. Treat your team (even if it's only you) as if it was your own business. Build brand-awareness; market and promote what you have to offer; and sell yourself, your team, and the profession.

Once you have raised the level of executive awareness, it's easier to position the need for an overall, business-driven content strategy overseen and managed at a senior level.

Why you need a CCO

Recall in the Introduction I stated that no matter what product or service your company or organization provides, or what need it is trying to fulfill, everyone, from the one-person consultancy to a multi-national mega-corporation, does the same five things:

1. Create something

Every company does something. They either create or improve on a product, or they develop and deliver a service. But these things don't just happen. They are often the result of extensive research and development efforts. Even if you don't have a formal R&D lab thinking up the best new mousetrap, as a business owner of any size you need to be constantly thinking about where your market is, how you can adapt to meet that market's needs, and hopefully how you can move into new markets. Development is an essential part of any company's operations.

2. Tell people about it

Once you have developed that thing that you do, it doesn't matter how great or revolutionary it is, you won't grow your company if you don't tell anyone about it. At one company I used to work for we used to joke that our new products weren't released, they just escaped. As a result revenue growth was flat. If you don't tell people about what you do, they won't be able to use your products. You need marketing.

3. Get people to buy it

If things are working well, when you start telling people about how great your mousetrap is, how it will solve their problem, and make their lives better, they will want to own one, or preferably several.And of course you would like them to keep buying newer versions of your mousetrap as you continue to develop them. This is where sales comes in. Whether you are a solo-business operator working the phones, or have a multi-national team of highly compensated sales executives, you still need to close the deal.

4. Collect money for it

Once you have developed, marketed and sold your mousetrap, I can imagine that you would really appreciate getting paid for it. Whether you work on a instant payment retail basis, or a credit based invoicing method, you need the money to flow. Money is the oil that lubricates any enterprise. You need it to cover your expenses, pay your staff, and if you manage things correctly, hopefully you will make a profit.

AND

5. Create content about it.

Every step of the way while doing those other four things you are also creating content about what you do. Everyone in your organizations does it. From the simplest of emails to complex policy and operation documents, to legal notices, to training courses, technical manuals, design specifications, manufacturing and servicing instructions. From websites to market collateral, sales brochures to proposal responses.The content you create about your product or service is often an essential and influential to the brand image of your company just as a commercial or advertisement would be. The collateral and content that support your product or service are an important part of customer interaction, satisfaction and overall customer experience.content is pervasive throughout your company and essential to every aspect of your business strategy and growth.

The previous chapters have shown that you content is your organization's biggest hidden asset. With a proper strategy, measurement, and management, it can reduce costs and increase revenue. And that means greater profits.

It's a success that everyone can contribute to.

However If everyone does it, then someone needs to manage it. If you have invested the time in understanding your content as an asset and developed a strategy to leverage it, then it needs to managed. Once you have business strategies, processes, goals, and key performance indicators assigned to the design, development, and distribution of your content, then someone needs to be accountable for ensuring those goals are meet and that the investments deliver the expected returns on investment.

As mentioned earlier, the other four key activities, design, marketing, sales, and finance, all have executive level accountability and oversight, so why not content? If your organization's intellectual property is contained in your content, then it is arguably just as important as the other four activities, if not more so. After all, where is the true worth of an organization if not in its intellectual property – the thing that makes it different from any other organization. To protect and manage that you need a content strategy, and for the content strategy to be truly effective it needs to be holistic and encompass the needs of the company as a whole. The broader the view, the higher the accountability.

 For a truly holistic view you need senior executive level accountability: in short, you need a CCO – A Chief Content Officer.

Acknowledgments

I've been swimming in The Content Pool for over twenty-five years, and during that time I've been lucky enough to work with a large number, and wide range, of talented people who have all contributed to my thoughts and ideas about how content can be used. There are way too many to name individually; but I would like to at least tip my metaphorical hat to my good friend, the late Gordon Farrington, my fellow editor in the early days of my career in the Technical Publications Department at British Aerospace, who first taught me to look at the content we produced as more than just words on paper.

In terms of this particular book project I'd like to thank XML Press Publisher, Richard Hamilton for listening to my pitch over dinner in Dallas during the 2009 STC Summit, and agreeing to help turn my ideas, experience, and stories into this book. Thanks to Mike Aragona, Rahel Anne Bailie, Anne Gentle, Larry Kunz, Mark Lewis, Leslie Paulson, and David Reeves for being such a great review team. All of them provided excellent notes, helped me overcome certain assumptions and preconceived ideas, and helped make the book a much better read. Special thanks to Leslie Paulson for writing the Foreword.

A particular vote of thanks goes to my friend, Doug Potter, for yet another great cover design and chapter title cartoons.

But, as always, the biggest vote of thanks goes to my family, my wonderful wife, Gill, and my two daughters, Meggan and Erin, for their support and encouragement, not just while writing this book, but throughout my career. Their willingness to move from one country to another, and across several different States, as I pursued new opportunities is only the tip of the support they have given me over the years. Thanks to them and to everyone who has joined me on this great journey across The Content Pool.

Alan J. Porter
Austin, TX
January, 2012

Bibliography

[1] Aberdeen Group. *Mobility in Service: The Agenda for 2010.* http://www.aberdeen.com/Aberdeen-Library/6339/RA-mobile-field-service.aspx. Available to subscribers to the Aberdeen Research Library.

[2] *Dictionary.com.* http://dictionary.reference.com/.

[3] Dunton-Downer, Leslie. *The English is Coming! How One Language is Sweeping the World.* Touchstone. 2010. ISBN: 978-1-4391-7665-6.

[4] Gentle, Anne. *Conversation and Community: The Social Web for Documentation.* XML Press. 2009. ISBN: 978-0-9822191-1-9.

[5] Gould, Jonathan. *Can't Buy Me Love: The Beatles, Britain and America.* Three Rivers Press. 2008. ISBN: 978-0307353382.

[6] Halvorson, Kristina. "The Discipline of Content Strategy." AlistApart.com. 2008. http://www.alistapart.com/articles/thedisciplineofcontentstrategy/ .

[7] Lovinger, Rachel. "Content Strategy: The Philosophy of Data." Boxes and Arrows. 2008. http://www.boxesandarrows.com/view/content-strategy-the.

[8] Maddox, Sarah. *Confluence, Tech Comm, Chocolate.* XML Press. 2012. ISBN: 978-1-937434-00-7.

[9] Mader, Stewart. *Wikipatterns.* Wiley, 2007, ISBN: 978-0470223628.

[10] McCloud, Scott. *Understanding Comics: The Invisible Art.* William Morrow Paperbacks. 1994. ISBN: 978-0060976255.

[11] McKee, Robert. *Story: Substance, Structure, Style and the Principles of Screenwriting.* It Books. 1997. ISBN: 978-0060391683.

[12] Pettegree, Andres. *The Book in the Renaissance.* Yale University Press. 2011. ISBN: 978-0300178210.

[13] Porter, Alan J. *Before They Were Beatles.* Xlibris. 2003. ISBN: 978-1413430561.

[14] Porter, Alan J. *James Bond: The History of the Illustrated 007.* Hermes Press. 2009. ISBN: 978-1932563184.

[15] Porter, Alan J. *WIKI: Grow Your Own for Fun and Profit.* XML Press. 2010. ISBN: 978-0-9822191-2-6.

[16] Porter, Alan J. *The James Bond Lexicon.* Hasslein Books. Coming in 2013.

[17] Powell, Lindsay. *All Things Under the Sun: How Modern Ideas are Really Ancient.* lulu.com. 2011. ISBN: 978-1257378708.

[18] Ressler, Sanford. *Perspectives on Electronic Publishing: Standards, Solutions, and More.* Prentice Hall. 1993. ISBN: 978-0132874915.

[19] Schriver, Karen A. *Dynamics in Document Design: Creating Text for Readers.* Wiley. 1996. ISBN: 978-0471306368.

[20] Sheffield, Richard. *The Web Content Strategist's Bible: The Complete Guide To A New And Lucrative Career For Writers Of All Kinds.* CreateSpace. 2009. ISBN: 978-1441482624.

[21] Smith, Douglas K. *Fumbling the Future.* iUniverse. 1999. ISBN: 978-1583482667.

[22] Straus, Jane. *The Blue Book of Grammar and Punctuation.* Graphics Pr. 2007. ISBN: 978-0470222683.

[23] Trumble, William R., editor. *Shorter Oxford English Dictionary*. Oxford University Press, USA. 2007. ISBN: 978-019923243. One of many editions of this venerable work.

[24] Tufte, Edward R. *The Visual Display of Quantitative Information*. Graphics Pr. 2001. ISBN: 978-0961392147. Second edition.

[25] *Websters Unabridged Dictionary*. http://www.gutenberg.org/ebooks/-29765 . Project Gutenberg's version of *Webster's Revised Unabridged Dictionary*, 1913 Edition, published by C. and G. Merriam Co., Springfield, Mass.

[26] *Merriam-Webster Online*. http://www.merriam-webster.com/.

[27] Wojcik, Richard H. and James E. Hoard. "Controlled Languages in Industry." In *Survey of the State of the Art in Human Language*, edited by Cole, Ronald, et al. Cambridge University Press. 2010. ISBN: 978-0521126243.

[28] Wurman, Richard Saul. *Information Architects*. Graphis Inc. 1997. ISBN: 978-1888001389.

[29] Wurman, Richard Saul. *Information Anxiety 2*. Que. 2000. ISBN: 978-0789724106. Follow up to his 1989 classic, *Information Anxiety*.

[30] Zambonini, Dan. "Content Strategists: What Do They Do?" Contentini.com. 2010. http://contentini.com/content-strategists-what-do-they-do/.

Index

A

B

C

About the Author

Alan J. Porter is an industry leading Content Strategist. He is currently engaged as a Senior Digital Publishing Consultant for PTC. He is also the President and Founder of 4Js Group LLC, a technical and business communications practice that specializes in applying creativity to meeting business needs and growth. He is a published author with several books, comics, and magazine articles to his name

In 2011 he was named as one of the Top Influencers in the Technical Communications industry.

You can find full details of Alan J. Porter's books as well as signing and speaking engagements at: http://alanjporter.com/

You can follow him on Twitter at @alanjporter[1] (for general writing and slice of life topics), or @4jsgroup[2] (for technical and content strategy topics).

THE CONTENT POOL, his blog on various thoughts and opinions on corporate communications, content strategy, and digital publishing can be found at http://thecontentpool.com[3]

---

[1] http://twitter.com/alanjporter
[2] http://twitter.com/4jsgroup
[3] http://thecontentpool.com/

About XML Press

XML Press (http://xmlpress.net) was founded in 2008 to publish content that helps technical communicators be more effective. Our publications support managers, social media practitioners, technical communicators, content strategists, and the engineers who support their efforts.

Our publications are available through most retailers, and discounted pricing is available for volume purchases for business, educational, or promotional use. For more information, send email to orders@xmlpress.net or call us at (970) 231-3624.

Related titles from XML Press

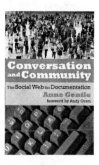

WIKI: Grow Your Own for Fun and Profit
by Alan J. Porter

Looking for a way to increase team collaboration, manage your company's knowledge? Do you need a way to manage projects with customers or suppliers outside your company firewall? Would you like your customers to provide feedback on the information you publish? Then a wiki might be just what you are looking for.

WIKI: Grow Your Own for Fun and Profit introduces wikis and shows how they are the must-have technology for collaboration and communication.

Conversation and Community
by Anne Gentle

Anne Gentle has been in the trenches working with the social web as a technologist and a community builder. Her book will help you understand the social web and will teach you techniques and best practices for working conversation and community into your documentation using tools like tag clouds, blogs, wikis, and syndication.

The second edition of this classic is coming in Spring 2012.

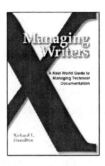

Confluence, Tech Comm, Chocolate
by Sarah Maddox

Web and Tech Comm guru Sarah Maddox takes you inside the Confluence wiki for an in-depth guide to developing and publishing technical documentation on a wiki.

In the words of wiki inventor Ward Cunningham, "Wiki wants you to work with others to incrementally write what will be incrementally read. Sarah wants you to approach this task with powerful tools and the confidence to wield them well. I want language and thought to find a happy home on the computer and look forward to our continuing progress together. And, of course, we all want chocolate."

Managing Writers
by Richard L. Hamilton

A practical guide to managing technical documentation projects in the real world, *Managing Writers* is for technical writers, both freelancers and employees, documentation managers, marketing managers and product development managers; anyone who may need to manage, full or part-time, a documentation project.

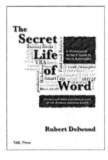

Learning Author-it
by Char James-Tanny

Let Author-it guru Char James-Tanny teach you how to get the most from Author-it. Char has taught hundreds in her acclaimed classes, and now she has drawn from her extensive experience to create the definitive resource for learning Author-it. Whether you are new to Author-it or an experienced user, there is something here for you.

The Secret Life of Word
by Robert Delwood

The Secret Life of Word looks at Microsoft Word from the perspective of technical and other professional writers. It gives you an insider's view of the hidden automation capabilities of Word.

This book will help you master the full gamut of Word mysteries, including AutoCorrect, QuickParts, BuildingBlocks, macros, Smart Tags, VBA basics, and much more. There's something here for everyone who uses Microsoft Word.

New in mid-2012

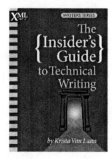

The Insider's Guide to Technical Writing

by Krista Van Laan

In 2001, Krista Van Laan and Catherine Julian published *The Complete Idiot's Guide to Technical Writing*. Now, Krista has completely updated the book and re-published it with XML Press as *The Insider's Guide to Technical Writing*. With a Foreword by JoAnn Hackos, *The Insider's Guide to Technical Writing* is the definitive reference for technical writers in the 21st century.

DITA Series

The long-anticipated XML Press DITA Series will launch with Eliot Kimber's *DITA for Practitioners* in May 2012. It will be followed by books about the DITA Open Toolkit, DITA Specialization, and DITA for writers. For the latest on the series, go to: http://xmlpress.net/publications/dita/

CPSIA information can be obtained at www.ICGtesting.com
Printed in the USA
BVOW05s0703120314

347409BV00010B/294/P